T0115369

The HISTORICAL EVOLUTION *of* CHRISTIAN WORSHIP

A Call to Worship

Mary R. Winters, D. Min, Ph.D.

WESTBOW
PRESS®
A DIVISION OF THOMAS NELSON
& ZONDERVAN

WestBow Press books may be ordered through booksellers or by contacting:

WestBow Press
A Division of Thomas Nelson & Zondervan
1663 Liberty Drive
Bloomington, IN 47403
www.westbowpress.com
844-714-3454

ISBN: 978-1-6642-2775-0 (sc)
ISBN: 978-1-6642-2776-7 (e)

Library of Congress Control Number: 2021905620

Print information available on the last page.

WestBow Press rev. date: 3/24/2021

Celebration of life
In memory of Mary R. Winters, Ph.D.
"Don't let life's tribulations root in your heart".

This book is dedicated to my Lord and Savior, Jesus Christ, who gave me the inspiration to write it. Without Him, this book would have been impossible.

I also dedicate this book to my husband, my daughter, my son-in-law, and my granddaughter—Dr. Virgil Winters, Jemiah, Tevin, and Maliyah—and my siblings: Linda, Faye, Gail, and Angeline.

Throughout my ministry and education, my family has been the rock on which I stand. They have supported me in all my endeavors. I have awaited their wisdom and looked to them for encouragement.

My husband is such a patient and understanding man. He has been the cornerstone in our family. I love you, honey, for thirty-eight years of marriage that seem like yesterday. I appreciate you for allowing me the time to do what God has ordained me to do.

I thank God for my wonderful parents, Thomas and Evangeline Roberson, who always saw something good in the things God was birthing out of me. They were always there to say, "Good job. We're praying for you!" Now, they're looking from heaven, and I hear the encouraging words they would always say.

PREFACE

Discussions regarding the evolution of man launch a specific direction of people's understanding on a regular basis. The political, global, and faith-based implications of its lessons sound clearly through the media. What is this great Christian nation to do, regarding such a publicized yet essential debate?

Do we clearly stand firm in the Christian belief that furnishes God as our sole creator and author of a complex world we call life? From a Christian perspective, the arguments are not easy, but the answers and truth are easily defined: "In the beginning, God created the heavens and the earth."

Evolution has been defined as the "development of life from lower to higher forms." How could a straightforward and forceful description be described in regard to the products of evolution?

As Christians describe evolution as God's creation, would the same developmental pattern be applicable to evolution's worship to its creator?

When did worship of God begin, and has it grown or diminished in its effect, value, and purpose? Does worship grow, or is it complete in its initial introduced form? What about the variation of worship among various cultures and religions?

Worship today has developed from a rich culture of combining worship of yesterday with how God is setting up worship for tomorrow. The appreciation for God is an ever-growing process, as we are simply individuals who are "not made but are being made every day." Simply stated, "Christian worship is a completed assignment with a growing work."

The procession, as preparation for worship, began in the fourth century. Worship in that century began to reflect local culture. This particularly was true of Eastern Christian worship. The Eastern worldview was informed by Hellenistic love for the appreciation of beauty. The contribution of this culture was poetry, literature, art, and philosophy. That worship, shaped by the Hellenistic imagination, is evident in the extensive use of ceremonial signs and symbols in Eastern worship.

In the praise-and-worship movement, the order of the service—the swing from praise to worship—is patterned after the movement in the Old Testament tabernacle and temple, from the outer court to the inner court and then into the holy of holies. All of these steps are accomplished through song.

In recent years, many contemporary churches, most of which were birthed out of the rise of the praise-and-worship tradition or influenced by the charismatic tradition, have introduced a whole new approach to the assembling of people for worship.

Because we are living in a time of transition in worship, it is important to pay careful attention to the acts of worship that assemble the people. There was a time when the pattern of assembling was predictable, but that is no longer true. As a congregation begins to develop a new pattern, it should keep in mind that the essential nature of the assembling of the people is a divine call and a human response. The entire experience of worship is a symbolic meeting with God, in which the eternal covenant, established by Jesus Christ, is reaffirmed in the physical action of worship. Therefore, Christians proclaim, by word and rite, Christ's death and Resurrection. They respond in faith with praise and thanksgiving. This is why worship necessitates forms and signs.

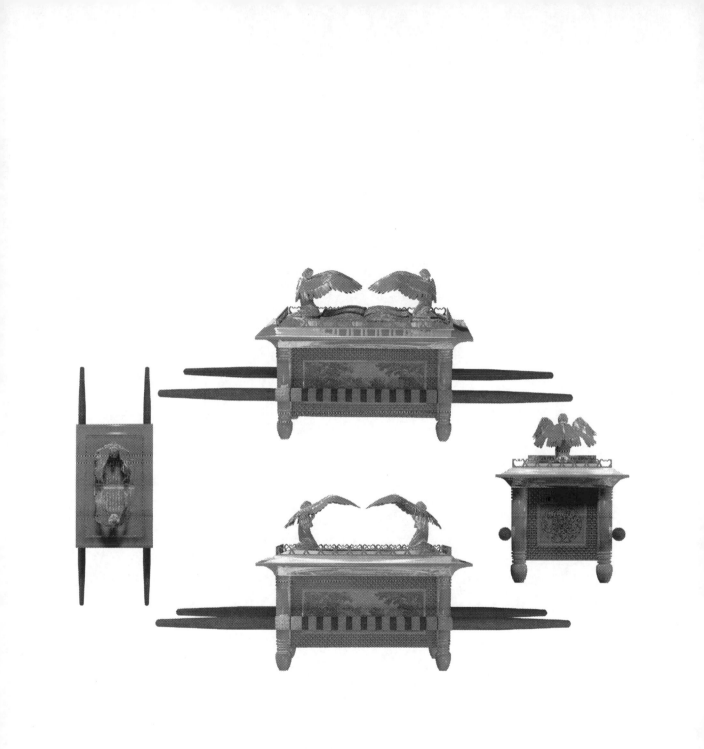

INTRODUCTION

The procession, as preparation for worship, began in the fourth century. Worship in that century began to reflect local culture. This particularly was true of Eastern Christian worship. The Eastern worldview was informed by the Hellenistic love for the aesthetic. They were sensitive to art and beauty. The contributions of this culture were poetry, literature, art, and philosophy. That worship, shaped by the Hellenistic imagination, is evident in the extensive use of ceremonial signs and symbols in Eastern worship.

In the praise-and-worship movement, the order of the service—the swing from praise to worship—is patterned after the movement in the Old Testament tabernacle and temple, from the outer court to the inner court and then into the holy of holies. All of these steps are accomplished through songs.

In recent years, many contemporary churches, most of which were birthed out of the rise of the praise-and-worship tradition or influenced by the charismatic tradition, have introduced a whole new approach to the assembling of people for worship.

Because we are living in a time of transition in worship, it is important to pay careful attention to acts of worship that assemble the people the people. There was a time when the pattern of assembling was predictable, but that is no longer true. As a congregation begins to develop new patterns, it should keep in mind that the essential nature of the assembling of the people is a divine call and a human response. The entire experience of worship is a symbolic meeting with God, in which the eternal covenant, established by Jesus Christ, is reaffirmed in the physical action of worship. Therefore, Christians proclaim, by word, Christ's death and Resurrection, and the way they respond by faith js with praise and thanksgiving. This is why worship necessitates forms and signs. It is also the way we connect with God through the Holy Spirit.

CHAPTER 1

The Nature of Worship

What is the nature of worship, as it relates to church music? Worship consists of rhythm, pitch, melody, and harmony, but it's not just that, for worship has power. Throughout the ages, people have been awed and mystified by the power of worship. During worship, the music that's provided brings changes of pitch, volume, tempo, rhythm, and harmony. It brings a wider variety of expressions than words. What seems intangible fades as soon as it is heard. What is different each time it's performed can express and elicit emotions of great intensity. It's something that touches the human soul.

Martin Luther views that "next to the Word of God, music deserves the highest praise." Music can comfort, excite encouragement, and call forth a host of other reactions, giving voice to unutterable feelings. It is a gift from God that encourages soundness of mind and enhances our lives. In the area of church music, it has played a prominent role in the service of Christian worship. It has accompanied every liturgical act from entrance rites to sacramental liturgies. It has been used to express every emotion, from grief to joy.

Music in worship is not an end in itself. It is a means by which the gospel is proclaimed and by which the people respond in prayer. It is the most universal way for rending Christian worship.

Mary R. Winters, D. Min, Ph.D.

What Is Worship?

The beauty and power of music and poetry provides a firm basis for worship and lends wings to communication between the human and the divine. Music also promotes the learning of words—by allowing more time for reflection than speech permits, by simply making words easier to memorize. Much about faith has been taught through the music of the church. All our worship traditions serve as a means of unifying the body of Christ. Singing binds people together as, with one heart, they lift their voices in praise. Worship is classified not as entertainment but as conversation. We hear the Word of God proclaimed and respond with praise and thanksgiving. It shows Christ's death until He comes again.

What is the difference between church music and concert music? The music performed in church is part of worship, not a concert program. Church music is not part of a concert, and the sermon is not an exercise in eloquent speaking. The Lord's Supper is not a snack served by people, paid with money received earlier during the service.

What's the difference between what happens in church and at a concert? The people are not an audience but a congregation. With hymns, psalms, and other worship music, the assembled congregation assumes the role of the orchestra. The primary purpose of worship music is to be a vehicle with which people praise God. Musicians occupy an important place in a community. Worship, in the praise-and-worship tradition, is based on the assumption that praise is not identical to worship. Praise is the prelude to worship and our entrance into God's presence. This is the point of true worship! The phrase "praise and worship" is frequently used by Christians but rarely are the words mentioned together in the Bible. *Webster's New World Dictionary* tells us that one meaning of the verb *praise* is "laud (to praise) the glory of God, as in song." Praise is God's idea, God's command, and God's pleasure. He loves to hear His people praising Him!

What is the difference between praise and worship? Worship encompasses thanksgiving, praise, and communion (commemorating the Last Supper), in which bread and wine are consecrated and consumed. Praise is born out of faith in God, an instrument of warfare, and a method of creating an atmosphere for the presence of the Lord. Worship is born from our relationship with God. We praise Him for what He has done and worship Him for who He is. Praise is a sacrifice that we give in faith and is our entrance into God's presence. Praise and worship have their own identities.

Day of Atonement

The Lord said to Moses, "The tenth day of this seventh month is the Day of Atonement. Hold a sacred assembly and deny yourselves and present a food offering to the Lord" (Leviticus 23:26–27 NIV).

To deny yourselves means to give up anything that will hinder you or interrupt you from something. When I went into ministry, the Lord God called me to deny myself and follow Him, to turn away from anything that would keep me from following Him. I had to repent of my sins and ask for forgiveness. My sins were atoned for by Jesus Christ. In the Old Testament, sins were atoned for by bulls, goats, and lambs. Now, the Lamb of God, Jesus Christ, takes away the sins of the world.

On Yom Kippur, Jews fast and express their regret for bad deeds during the past year and their hope to perform good deeds in the coming year. According to tradition, Yom Kippur is the day on which Moses descended from Mount Sinai with the second tablets of stone, forty days after the collective sin of the golden calf.

Yom Kippur is the Jewish Day of Atonement and is the most important and sacred Jewish holy day. Jews observe Yom Kippur as a day of fasting and worship. On this day, devout Jews think of their sins, repent, and ask forgiveness from God and from other people. In ancient times, the high priest held a service in Jerusalem and sacrificed certain animals as a ceremonial offering. The service part of the process of repentance and atonement was the main event of the day. Today, Jews fast, perform no work, and attend services in the temple. Yom Kippur is found in Leviticus 16; 23:26–32; 25:9 and Numbers 29:7–11.

Scapegoat

On the Day of Atonement, one of two goats received by the Jewish high priest in ancient Jerusalem was a scapegoat. One was for Yaweh (Jehovah), the Hebrew God, and was killed as a sacrificial offering. The second was called the scapegoat. The priest lay his hands upon the scapegoat as he confessed the people's's sins. Then the priest sent the scapegoat into the wilderness. This was a symbol that indicated the sins had been forgiven. Today, a person who has been blamed for something that is the fault of another is referred to as a scapegoat. We all have seen, one way or another, someone taking the blame for someone else and have known it wasn't the scapegoat's fault.

Fasting Relating to Judaism and Christianity

There are important fast days in Judaism and Christianity. Jewish law orders a yearly fast on Yom Kipper, the Day of Atonement. Many Orthodox Jews follow the custom of having the bride and groom fast on the day before their wedding. Many Christians fast during Lent, the period of forty days from Ash Wednesday until Easter, commemorating the forty days that Jesus spent fasting in the wilderness.

For Christians, fasting seldom means doing without all food for an entire day. People who are not well can usually receive permission from their religious leaders or doctors to not fast. Fasting is abstinence from food or certain kinds of food for a certain period. The custom of fasting has played a part in the practices of every major religious group at some time.

I have fasted for many reasons. It often has been a way that I've sought pardon for my deeds. I have fasted many times when families were in the hospital or couples wanted children. I've fasted for debt cancellation, marriages, breaking generational curses, and so on. The custom of fasting has had a part in the practices of every major religious group at some time. There are many purposes for fasting. It often has been a way that people have sought pardon for their sins.

In some religions, people fast during times of mourning. In others, people believe that fasting will take their minds away from physical things and produce a state of spiritual joy and happiness. People also have fasted for health reasons. Scientist have studied the effects of fasting on the body and found that food intake increases the body's metabolism. After fasting, metabolism can be as much as 22 percent lower than the normal rate. But research also has shown that after long periods of fasting, the body tends to adjust by lowering the rate of metabolism itself.

When I fast, I gradually resume eating. There have been times when I didn't and felt the effects of it! Fasting is not intended to be harmful. It does promote self-control and strengthens the will.

Feasts and Festivals

In Judaism, the two most sacred festivals are Rosh Hashanah, which is the Jewish New Year, and Yom Kippur, the Day of Atonement. According to Jewish tradition, people are judged on Rosh Hashanah for their deeds of the past year. On Yom Kippur, Jews fast, express their regret for past sins, and declare their hope of performing good deeds during the coming year. These are also known as High Holidays, and like all Jewish holidays, they occur on different dates each year because they are based on the Hebrew calendar. The High Holidays come during Tishri, the first month of the Hebrew calendar, which usually falls in September or October.

Hebrew Calendar

The Hebrew calendar begins with an estimated moment of the world's creation. Hebrew tradition has placed this moment at 3,760 years and three months before the birth of Jesus Christ. To find a year in the Hebrew calendar, we must add 3,760 to the date in the Gregorian calendar. For example, the year 2000 in the Gregorian calendar is the year 5760 in the Hebrew calendar. This system, however, will not work to the exact month because the Hebrew year begins in September or October in the Gregorian calendar. The Hebrew calendar is based on the moon and normally consists of twelve months: Tishri, Heshvan, Kislev, Tebet, Shebat, Adar, Nisan, Iyar, Sivan, Tammuz, Ab, and Elul. They are alternately thirty and twenty-nine days long. Seven times during every nineteen-year period, an extra twenty-nine–day month, called Veadar, is inserted between Adar and Nisan. At the same time, Adar is given thirty days instead of twenty-nine. These additions keep the Hebrew calendar and holidays in agreement with the seasons of the solar year.

Synagogue

Synagogue is the Jewish house of worship and the center of Jewish education and social life. The word *synagogue* usually refers to the place where worship and other activities take place. The synagogue has become one of the most important centers for the transmission and reservation of Judaism. A synagogue has many functions. People gather there for worship services every morning and evening, as well as on the Sabbath and on holy days. Synagogues have schools, where children and adults study the scriptures, the Hebrew language, and Jewish history. Important events, such as a wedding or a Bar Mitzvah, are celebrated in the synagogue. In the United States, many synagogues also serve as meeting places for Jewish organizations in the community.

Jews began to gather for formal prayer in biblical times at the temple in Jerusalem, when it was the center of Jewish life. The temple was destroyed in 587 or 586 BC. Later, buildings called synagogues were built. They served as places of prayer and study and as centers of Jewish life worldwide.

The synagogue is the Jewish house of worship and the center of Jewish education and community activities. A synagogue has a sanctuary, where religious services are held. It may also include a school, where children study Judaism, Hebrew language and Jewish history. Most synagogues have social hall as well. Reform Conservative synagogues are often called temples. Most synagogues are constructed so that the worshippers face toward the holy city of Jerusalem during the service. At the front of the sanctuary stands the ark, a chest in which the scrolls of the Torah are kept. In front of the ark hangs the eternal light—an oil lamp, the constant flames of which symbolize God's eternal presence.

The Cantor

The cantor chants the prayers during worship in the synagogue. The cantor is often a professional who has a trained voice and special knowledge of Hebrew and the traditions of chanting. The cantor may also direct a choir and conduct religious education.

The Rabbi

The rabbi serves as spiritual leader, teacher, and interpreter of Jewish law. Traditionally, rabbis were chiefly teachers of the Law. Today, rabbis also deliver sermons during worship services in the synagogue, give advice to people with problems, and perform other functions. A person who wants to become a rabbi must spend years studying Hebrew sacred writings and Jewish history, philosophy, and law. Most rabbinical students also study a wide range of nonreligious subjects. In the United States, Orthodox rabbis are trained at Yeshiva University and other rabbinical seminaries; Reform rabbis at the Hebrew Union College; and Conservative rabbis at the Jewish Theological Seminary of America.

Mary R. Winters, D. Min, Ph.D.

Worship

Worship in Judaism takes place in the home and the synagogue. Important parts of home worship include daily prayers, the lighting of the Sabbath candles, and the blessing of the wine and bread at the Sabbath meal. Jews also observe many holiday rituals at home. Worship practices in the synagogue differ among the branches of Judaism and even within these groups. Orthodox and Conservative synagogues conduct services daily, but most Reform synagogues have services only on the Sabbath and holidays. In all Orthodox and some Conservatives synagogues, at least ten men must be present for a service to take place. This minimum number of participants is called a *minyan*. Any male who is at least thirteen years old may lead service. In most Conservative and Reform congregations, women may lead the service and be part of the minyan.

Synagogue worship consists mainly of reading from the Torah and chanting prayers from a prayer book, called the *siddur*. A different portion of the Torah is read each week, so the entire Torah is completed in a year. In Orthodox synagogues, men and women sit separately and chant almost all the prayers in Hebrew. In Conservative and Reform congregations, men and women sit together, and much of the service is in the language of the country. Most Sabbath and holiday services include a sermon. Did you know you are not suppose to wear leather shoes on Yom Kippur? Remember: Yom Kippur is the Jewish Day of Atonement and one of the most important and sacred Jewish holy fays.

The *World Book Encyclopedia* references Jesus in the Jewish Feast of Yom Kippur. The dictionary definition of *atonement* is "the act or fact of making up for something, giving satisfaction for a wrong, loss or injury; amends; reconciliation, harmony; Day of Atonement or the reconciliation of God with sinners through the sufferings and death of Christ.

"Through our Lord Jesus Christ, through whom we have now received reconciliation" (Romans 5:11 NIV).

The Yom Kippur holiday falls on the tenth day of the month of Tishri in the Jewish calendar (in September or October). It is the culmination of the observance of the Ten Days of Penitence, which begin with Rosh Hashanah, the New Year, and is the most sacred of Jewish holidays. Yom Kippur is a day of confession, repentance, and prayers for forgiveness of sins committed during the year against God's law and covenant. It is also the day on which an individual's fate for the ensuing year is thought to be sealed.

Jews observe the day by a rigorous fast and nearly unbroken prayer. It is required by law for all Jews to fast on Yom Kippur, except those who are ill or children younger than age thirteen. The aim of this fast is concentration on the congregation's relationship to God. During this day are five sermons with confessions and prayers for forgiveness from God.

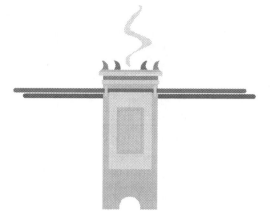

CHAPTER 2
Proponents of Worship

The Origin

The Bible tells us that in the beginning, there was the Word, and the Word was with God, and the Word was God. The same was in the beginning with God. All things were made by Him, and without Him was not anything made that was made. In Him was life, and the life was the light of men, and the light shone in darkness, and the darkness comprehended it not. There was a man sent from God, whose name was John. The same came for a witness, to bear witness of the light; that all men through Him might believe. He was not that light but was sent to bear witness of that light. That was the true light, which lighted every man who came into the world. He was in the world, and the world was made by him, and the world knew Him not.

God is love, and God is holy. Because love is His predominant characteristic, God desired to surround His throne with creatures whom He might love and by whom He might be loved. Because of His holiness, these creatures must also be holy. By logical necessity, love and holiness cannot be forced. These loving and holy creatures must be endowed with the ability to choose whether to glorify God and to enjoy Him forever or to reject Him and suffer the consequences. God's first people the universe, a hierarchy of holy angels, of whom one of the highest orders was the cherubim. One of them, the anointed cherub, was the closest to God. This cherub was created beautiful and perfect in his ways. He knew that he was beautiful, but pride entered his heart, and the first sin in the entire history of eternity occurred. Pride led to self-will, and self-will to rebellion. This great cherub became the adversary of God, Satan, and led other angels into rebellion. God then created man in His own image, to worship Him, with the possibility of becoming holy on condition of obedience. Angels are supernatural or heavenly beings, a little higher in dignity than man. They were created before man. The work of the angels varies. Good angels stand in the presence of God and worship Him. They assist, protect, and deliver God's people.

Of the origin of religion, it's often been said that it's a matter of guesswork. The first creatures that stood erect must still have been animals at heart. We know that animals do not have a religion. We also know that two thousand years ago, by the time of Jesus Christ, man had attained a very high form of religion. Therefore, in between there must have been a gradual evolution of religion upwards to the higher forms.

The next step in the evolution of Christian worship is to assume that the lower forms of religion must have been something like Stone Age tribes, which were untouched by modern civilization. They didn't have the opportunity to meet God in their wilderness. They had not known the God of Abraham, Isaac, and Jacob. These tribal people worshipped spirits of the dark and relied on witch doctors to practice magic. Witch doctors eventually became priests, with sacrifices and temples and books of ritual.

The next step is that, eventually, worship dawned on people—that loving one's neighbor as you love yourself is the main thing in religion, and the one who first taught that clearly was Jesus, who founded Christian worship.

The Beginning of Humankind

According to the Bible, in the beginning, God created the heavens and the earth. On the sixth day of creation, God said, "Let us make human beings in our image and in our likeness." God created male and female. He blessed them and said to them, "Be fruitful and multiply. Fill the earth and subdue it. Rule over the fish in the sea and the birds in the sky and over every living creation on the ground, every seed-bearing plant and everything that has the breath of life" (Genesis 1:26–31 NIV). God created human beings to worship Him.

Scientists think that humans evolved from lower forms; there truly had to be a first male and first female. They had to be able to propagate a race of humans. What were these first truly human beings like? Were they half-stooping, gorilla-faced cave-dwellers, beginning the long ascent to civilization? The Bible is silent on this. We are not told whether they were black or white, stooped or erect, tall or small, or with snubs. We are given the basic facts concerning their nature—the first human couple, male and female, was made from dust of the earth. What made the first couple distinct from all the animals was that they were made in the image of God. Man is not like God in His shape or almighty power or His ability to be in more than one place at one time; man is not all-knowing. But one thing that the image of God in man does imply is that man can understand and choose to listen to the voice of God.

The Beginning of Worship

In looking for the origin of worship, we begin with humans who could respond to God's voice. At first, they presumably loved Him with all their hearts and also loved each other. By the third and fourth chapters of Genesis, we find that this first love for God and for one another suffered by sin. In that first state, humans did not need temples or priests; no sacrifice arose. In Genesis 4, we find Cain bringing an offering of fruits of the ground and Abel bringing an animal sacrifice. Abel's animal sacrifice was accepted by God, but Cain's offering of fruit was rejected, for God knew their motives. One way was shown by which sinful man could approach a holy God; the other way was the shedding of blood, which is death. At first, the head of the family or tribe would preside in the offering of sacrifice.

After the exodus from Egypt, Moses appointed a special line of priests, descended from Aaron, to supervise the morning and evening, weekly, monthly, and special sacrifices. Later, in the time of Solomon, a temple was built for the same purpose, and the offering of an animal sacrifice among the Jews continued until AD 70, forty years after the death of Christ. There was nothing particularly primitive or barbaric about animal sacrifice. In our cities, thousands of animals are slaughtered every day for food. In the Old Testament period, each killing of an animal was given a religious meaning, and that meaning became only fully clear in the death of Jesus Christ on the cross.

The Development of Religion

According to the Bible, the first religion of man was monotheism—belief in one God—and animal sacrifice indicated that there was a way of forgiveness and acceptance before him. This helps us to understand the subsequent history of religion. The Old Testament gives examples of how, again and again, men were tempted from monotheism (worship of one God) into polytheism (worship of more than one God).

Priestcraft and Magic

There is a constant temptation to change God's gracious provision of sacrifice into a ritual that has value only in itself. The priests of Egypt and Greece claimed that their sacrifices were pleasing to God and could obtain blessings for the worshippers. This false view, not sacrifice in itself, is what the great prophets of Israel spoke against. Priestcraft is only one step into magic and the religion of the tribal witch doctors.

There is a constant process of degeneration of religion into the lower forms of polytheism, priestcraft, and magic. Abraham's call from the idolatry and magic of Ur of the Chaldees to worship the one true God with a simple faith based on god's way of sacrifice. Later, Moses had to teach the children of Israel, who had been corrupted in Egypt, to worship the one true God and to offer sacrifice in a way that is clear that no magic was intended.

Maintaining True Worship

The Bible illustrates the historical process of the decline of worship and the sending of prophets to restore and reform true worship. On the night before Jesus died, He provided the symbols of bread and wine with His disciples, which reminds us of his final sacrifice. We are told in the Bible that Jesus said that as often as we drink the cup and eat the bread, we show the Lord's death until He comes.

Among the Jews and among other nations, the practice of animal sacrifice ceased. This did not end the decline of worship. In the Christian Church and in religions such as Hinduism, priests claim that their rituals can force God to give favors in this life and the next.

The Bible and Anthropology

Anthropology is the study of human societies and cultures and their development. It is also the study of human biological and physiological characteristics and their evolution.

Since the worship of one God, based on animal sacrifice, leaves no evidence for archeologists, we should be suspicious of attempts to reconstruct primitive religion by guesswork, based on a few skulls and cave drawings.

Long before Abraham, the ancient Egyptians, Sumerians, and people of the Indus Valley civilization in India were building temples and using idols. These religions indicate that the process of degeneration had already taken place, and Abraham's task was to restore true worship, not take an upward step in its evolution.

In the sixth century BC, Buddha, the founder of Buddhism, taught that man could attain salvation by his own efforts. Buddhists rejected the practice of animal sacrifice and, in fact, recommended vegetarianism. They were right in objecting to the priestly magic, but they did not understand God's way of forgiveness. It is often assumed that the Stone Age tribes were discovered in the last hundred years and give us examples of original primitive religion. Research suggests that primitive tribes have a memory of a "high god" who is fatherly and good. Also, growing evidence shows that the sacrifice of witch doctors was a decline from higher forms, rather than a remnant of primitive worship.

The patriarchs—Abraham and the rest—were semi-nomads. They moved from place to place instead of living in one place. They lived in tents and moved about with their families, flocks, and herds in search of fresh pasture and water. After the exodus, the people of Israel settled in their

Promised Land. From that time through the rise of kings and the division of kingdoms, the life of ordinary people followed a pattern that changed little.

Why Worship?

Ceremonial processions, including dance, were a feature of the festival of Israel worship. The festal march symbolized God's reign over Israel and presented the picture of an army following its king into war.

In Israel's worship, processions around the walls of Jericho began the conquest of Canaan, a ceremonial act that took place in actual warfare, according to Joshua 6. A company of musicians and worshippers led the armies of Jehoshaphat into battle. and afterward, they marched back into Jerusalem, carrying their instruments and rejoicing in the Lord's victory on their behalf.

According to 2 Chronicle 20, Jehoshaphat told the people to have faith in the Lord, their God. He reminded them that they would be upheld and to have faith in God's prophets, for they would be successful. He appointed men to sing to the Lord and praise Him for the splendor of his holiness as they went out at the head of the army, saying, "Give thanks to the Lord, for his Love endures forever" (2 Chronicle 20:20–21 NIV).

The Gospels describe a procession similar to those found in the Old Testament, with one difference. Instead of being led by the ark, the symbol of God's presence, this procession centers around Jesus Christ Himself, riding on a donkey, surrounded with songs of worshippers waving palm branches and shouting, "Hosanna!" or "Save us, Lord!" This celebration pictures the crowning of a sovereign Christ as king of Israel.

The psalms contain, in miniature, the whole of God's covenant dealings with His people in a form that speaks directly from heart to heart. The psalms have been called "the prayer book of the Bible" because they are poems of worship. The psalms give praise, thanks, petitions, and curses and tell stories, employing a variety of structures and techniques along the way. In every period of Israel's and the church's life, the psalms have been employed in worship and regarded as indispensable.

The Importance of the Psalms

The book of Psalms is also considered as the book of praises. It is one of the major portions of the holy scripture. In the Hebrew Bible, it's at the beginning of the third division of the canon, the "Writings," after the Law and the prophets. The three Old Testament books most often quoted in the New Testament are Deuteronomy (from the Law), Isaiah (from the prophets), and Psalms. The apostles saw the psalms as prophetic of Christ. They followed the lead of Jesus Himself, who, in appearing to His disciples after the Resurrection, had reminded them, "Everything must be fulfilled that is written about me in the Law of Moses, the Prophets and the Psalms" (Luke 24:44 NIV).

Customarily, David bears the authorship of the psalms. The psalms are conventional worship texts that adapt to the needs of the community. The prophetic voice that often speaks in the psalms reflects their development through the work of the Leviticus musicians of the sanctuary. It is often said that the psalms are the voice of the worshipper, calling out to God, rather than the Word of God directed to His people. The psalms are a dialogue, for God speaks in them as well. The psalms are organized in five books.

The organization of the book of Psalms reflects the growth of the collection in several stages. The superscriptions of many Psalms contain information relevant to their collection and performance. These books probably correspond to five books of the Pentateuch, or Law of Moses.

The divisions within the psalms are:

Book I—Psalms 1–41
Book II—Psalms 42–72
Book III—Psalm 73–89
Book IV—Psalm 90–106
Book V—Psalms 107–150

Each of the first four books ends with a doxology, and Psalm 150 serves as the doxology to the entire collection. The first psalm, which describes the righteous worshipper who delights in the law of the Lord, serves as an introduction to the psalms.

Here I Am to Worship

A new style of worship that started spreading throughout North America and other parts of the world is the praise-and-worship movement, which has proceeded from the traditional worship forms of a dead church to a live church. There was a concern for the immediacy of the Spirit, a desire for intimacy.

It must be persuaded that music and informality must connect with people of a post-Christian culture. There were testimonial songs, such as, "He Touched Me," "There's Something about the Name of Jesus," "Because He Lives, I Can Face Tomorrow," "Great Is Your Mercy towards Me," "I Am a Friend of God," "Every Praise Is to Our God," and "My God Is an Awesome God," as examples. These songs touched many lives, including my own. It introduced us to a new type of music that consoled us in our time of need. Whether we needed comfort from the passing of our parents, children moving from home, healing in our bodies, lifting our burdens, or seeking God for answers during the coronavirus (COVID-19), singing songs of praise and thanksgiving in worship has been our answer for healing, recovery, restoration, deliverance, and peace. This developed into a new approach to worship. Praise and worship seeks to recapture the lost element of praise found in both the Old and New Testaments. The proponents of praise and worship say, "Praise God first and foremost, and then move on to the other elements of worship."

Psalm 95:1–7 invites us for worship. It's a prelude to worship. It's not an attempt to get something from God but what we offer to Him. We offer praise for what He has done, for His mighty deeds in history, and His continued presence in our lives.

> Come, let us sing for joy to the Lord; Let us shout aloud to the Rock of our salvation. Let us come before him with thanksgiving and extol him with music and song. For the Lord is the great God, the great King above all gods. In His hand are the depths of the earth and the mountain peaks belong to Him. The sea is His, for He made it, and His hands formed the dry land. Come, let us bow down in worship, let us kneel before the Lord our Maker; for He is our God and we are the people of His pasture, the flock under His care. (Psalm 95:1–7 NIV)

The Order of Service

The swing from praise to worship is patterned after the Old Testament tabernacle and temple, from the outer court to the inner court and then into the holy of holies. Through songs, the worship leader moves the congregation through various steps that lead to worship.

First, choruses begin with personal experience or testimony, such as, "This Is the Day the Lord Has Made," or "We Bring Sacrifices of Praise into the House of the Lord." The upbeat songs are centered on praise and relate to the personal experience of the believer.

In the second step, the mood and content of the music shift to express the action of entering the gates and coming into the courts. The worship leader leads people in songs that express the transition from praise to worship, such as, "Make a joyful noise unto the Lord!" (Psalm 100:1–5 KJV).

The third step is into the holy of holies, which brings believers away from themselves and into a fully conscious worship of God alone. No longer is the worshipper thinking about what God has done but rather of who God is, in person and character. A quiet devotion hovers over the congregation as they sing songs such as, "I Love You, Lord," and "You Are Worthy." Clapping likely will be replaced with responses of upturned faces, raised hands, tears, and a subtle change in the voices. This is described as an experience of "the manifest presence of God." Can you see this experience of the presence of Christ at the Lord's Table? In this atmosphere is where the spiritual gifts are released, and many taste the special manifestations of the Holy Spirit in worship, according to Psalm 22:3.

The most distinction of a typical service is that of praise from worship. Some acts in the service include the time for teaching, intercessory prayers, and ministry. Most praise-and-worship churches are informal. Intercessory prayer may be informal. A prayer circle may replace the traditional pastoral prayers. The time of ministry may be in different rooms. Some traditional churches may be unaware or ignorant of the praise-and-worship movement. Some traditional churches actively dismiss praise and worship, arguing that they are "too charismatic." Then, some traditional churches are not only aware of praise and worship but seek to integrate this new approach to worship into the local church.

Holiness—Pentecostal Worship

Pentecostal worship began with the Azuza Street Revival of 1906 in Los Angeles. The Holy Spirit fell upon a group of worshippers and gifted them with the ability to speak in tongues. This movement traces its origin to John Wesley and his conviction that a conversion experience should be followed by a second work of God's grace. Some insisted that a second work of sanctifying grace should be a part of everyone's Christian experience. The people sought this holiness experience, gathering in camp meetings to hear teachings and sing, through agonizing prayer, through to the second work of grace. They had a freedom in worship, accompanied by shouting when they "broke through" and experienced sanctifying grace. People would weep and wail, groan out loud, and enter a near-convulsive state as they sought God. Worship among Pentecostals was characterized by freedom, spontaneity, individual expression, and joy. Cultural music was used to present the gospel. The songs told stories of how people came to faith and received Jesus, such as, "I came to Jesus weary, worn, and sad." In their worship, they included stringed instruments, organs, and drums.

Another feature of worship is praying and singing in the Spirit. This kind of prayer is more than spirited, directed prayer; it is an actual Spirit-given language known as tongues. Tongues may occur in two different forms.

First, in some cases, a message may be given in tongues. During this time, a hush falls over the congregation, and everyone listens to the messages in tongues. It is followed by interpretation, through which the message given by God in another language was communicated in the language of the people and to the people.

A second form of tongues is understood only by God. In these times of prayer directed by the worship leader or occurring spontaneously after a song, no interpretation is made, for tongues, in this instance, is not a message from God to the peopl but a personal prayer language.

Prophecies are unique to worship. It is a message given by a person for the purpose of strengthening, encouraging, or comforting the worshippers. The Bible says, "But those who prophecy, speak to people for their up building and encouragement and consolation. Those who speak in tongues edify themselves, but those who prophesy edify the Church" (1 Corinthians 14:3–4 NIV).

While we praise God for what He has done, we worship God for who He is—the person and character of God. Through songs, the worship leader moves the congregation through various steps that lead to worship.

CHAPTER 3
Tabernacle of Moses

The primary purpose of the tabernacle was to provide God with a place to dwell in the midst of Israel. Exodus 25:8 says, "And let them make me a sanctuary; that I may dwell among them" (KJV).

The ark of the covenant is the object that is very full of spiritual teaching in the various incidents in its history, as we follow it through the wilderness and the Jordan to Gilgal, around the walls of Jericho, to Shiloh, then to the land of the Philistines, and back again through Beth Shemesh, Kiriath-Jearim, and the house Obed-Edom of, until it finally rests in its place in the tent in Jerusalem and in the temple of Solomon. The history of the nation was intimately connected with the history of the ark. If it was in captivity, they were in trouble and distress, but when it occupied its rightful place, they were prosperous and happy. The ark of the covenant foreshadows the Lord Jesus Christ. There is no doubt as to its being a type of Jesus. The purpose for which it was made proves this, for God said to Moses, "There I will meet with thee, and I will commune with thee from above the Mercy-seat" (Exodus 25:22 KJV). We read in Romans 3 oof Him, "whom God hath set forth to be a propitiation or mercy-seat through faith in His blood" (Roman 3:25 KJV). He himself is the thrones of graced, where God meets with the sinner. He is God's meeting place with man.

The name *Jesus* is not here, used alone to speak to us of His life of humiliation on earth, nor is it put first, still emphasizing His character as the suffering one, but it is, "The Man in the Glory" that is now the "Mercy-seat," where we may obtain mercy for the past and grace for the present and future.

The purpose of the altar of burnt offering and part of the tabernacle was to lift up high or ascend.

> The Lord is God, and he has made his light shine on us. With boughs in hand, join in the festal procession up to the horns of the altar. You are my God and I will praise you; you are my God and I will exalt you. Give thanks to the Lord, for he is good; his love endures forever. (Psalm 118:27–29 NIV)

> Oh give thanks unto the Lord; for he is good: because his mercy endureth forever. … I called upon the Lord in distress: the Lord answered me, and set me in a large place. The Lord is on my side; I will not fear: what can man do unto me? … It is better to trust in the Lord than to put confidence in man. (Psalm 118:1, 5-6, 8 KJV)

It was these horns onto which the sacrificial animals were tied. The sacrifices of the Old Testament were unwilling sacrifices, but Jesus Christ came as our New Testament sacrifice, once and for all. He was a willing sacrifice that did not have to be tied. He was only bound by a love to do His Father's will.

When Jesus came into the world, He said that sacrifice and offering—burnt offerings and sin offerings—you did not desire, nor were you pleased with them; therefore, He has come only to do the will of the Father. We have been made holy through the sacrifice of the body of Jesus Christ, once and for all.

According to John 3:16, "For God so loved the world, that he gave his only begotten Son, that whosoever believeth in him should not perish, but, have everlasting life" (KJV).

Jesus reminds us that He is the Good Shepherd; the Good Shepherd gives His life for His sheep. The sheep belong to Jesus, just as the Father knows Him, so He knows the Father, and He lays down His life for His sheep. His Father loves Him because He lays His life down and takes it up again.

Jesus says, "No man taketh it from me, but I lay it down of myself. I have power to lay it down and I have power to take it again. This commandment have I received of my Father" (John 10:18 KJV).

Coming Out to the Outer Court

In coming out to the outer court, we find that the brazen altar was placed before the door or at the "foot," the beginning of man's approach to God.

And thou shalt set the altar of the burnt offering before the door of the tabernacle of the tent of the congregation. (Exodus 40:6 KJV)

And he put the altar of burnt offering by the door of the tabernacle, of the tent of the congregation and offered upon it the burnt offering and the meat offering; as the Lord commanded Moses. (Exodus 40:29 KJV)

Jesus Christ was lifted up on the cross, His altar. Since then, He has ascended up and is high above all. *Altar* means "slaughter place or sacrifice," to the Hebrew understanding. In the Greek, it carries the thought of being "a place for the slaying and burning of victims." Calvary was indeed the slaughter place. Christ was led, as a lamb to the slaughter, and flayed alive for us. The altar pointed to Calvary's cross, where all that the brazen altar foreshadowed was fulfilled.

The Purpose of the Laver and the Part of the Tabernacle

Moses was instructed to make a laver, which was to be set in the courtyard (outer court) between the tent of the tabernacle (congregation) and the brazen altar. The priests would wash their hands in the top, or large basin. Whatever the case, the vessel's chief function was to supply the water for the cleansing of the priests. This is sanctification. The laver was used especially to cleanse the priests for ministry.

And thou shalt set the Laver between the Tent of the congregation and the altar and shalt put water therein. (Exodus 40:7 KJV)

And he set the Laver between the Tent of the congregation and the altar and put water there to wash withal. (Exodus 40:30 KJV)

The Tabernacle of Moses Consists of Many Sections

The tabernacle of Moses was simply a portable tent with various curtains and coverings over a wooden structure. It had three apartments, or places, to it. The scripture refers to each of these:

- The holiest of all, or most holy place
- The holy place
- The outer court

> What was the purpose of the table of shewbread, altar of incense, and the golden candlestick? What section of the tabernacle were they in?

The table of shewbread was placed in the sanctuary directly opposite the golden candlestick in the holy place. It was placed on the north side of the tabernacle.

> And he put the table in the tent of the congregation upon the side of the Tabernacle northward, without the vail. (Exodus 40:22 KJV)

When man falls, communion with God is broken. In Exodus, we are given a picture of fallen man, redeemed by the grace of God. We see God's grace coming to fallen man to reestablish the severed lines of communion.

God provides the table for His priests in the sanctuary. All of this puts forth the truth that God has prepared a table in Christ for His redeemed people, the priests of the eternal Sanctuary.

The table of shewbread is significant of the Lord Jesus Christ Himself, as the bread of life to His people, and it points to the table of the Lord or the Communion of the New Testament church, the body of Christ. This table is what David had in mind when he declared, "Thou preparest a table before me in the presence of mine enemies" (Psalms 23:5 KJV).

It would take the light of the golden candlestick to reveal and illuminate the bread and the table. The golden candlestick was positioned immediately opposite the golden table on the south side of the holy place in the sanctuary. The golden candlestick was a lampstand on which were seven lighted lamps, not candles. Candles burn by self-consumption, while lamps burn by the continual supply of oil being poured into them.

The church is not merely to be a candle or to give candlelight; it is to be a lampstand, shedding forth divine light by the continual supply of the oil of the Holy Spirit. The chief purpose of the lampstand was to give light and to illuminate all that was in the sanctuary.

Notice several allusions to the candlestick, from the time it was constructed in the wilderness to the time when it was used at Belshazzar's feast, and the handwriting of judgment was seen "over against the candlestick." This was a solemn warning against that which had been dedicated to service of the Lord being used for other purposes.

The golden altar of incense was for the burning of incense unto the Lord. Incense always speaks to us of the prayers and intercession of the saints who ascend unto God. Incense begins on the altar with man, and as it burns, it ascends upward to God. Likewise, our prayers begin in the heart of man and ascend heavenward unto God. The altar of incense was placed in the holy place.

> Lord, I cry unto thee: make haste unto me, give ear unto my voice, when I cry unto thee. Let my prayer be set forth before thee as incense; and the lifting up of my hands as the evening sacrifice. (Psalm 141:1–2 KJV)

> And I saw the seven angels which stood before God; and to them were given seven trumpets and another Angel came and stood at the altar, having a golden censer;

and there was given unto him much incense, that he should offer it with prayers of all saints upon the golden altar which was before the throne. And the smoke of the incense, which came with the prayers of the saints, ascended up before God out of the Angel's hand. And the Angel took the censer and filled it with fire of the altar and cast it into the Earth and there were voices and thundering and lightning and an earthquake. And the Seven Angels which had the Seven Trumpets prepared themselves to sound. (Revelation 8:2–6 KJV)

Incense is all that was to be burned upon the golden altar in the holy place. This is because the outer court was the place of sacrifice.

➢ What is the purpose of the ark of the covenant? What part of the tabernacle was it located?

The ark of the covenant was made of shittim wood, overlaid with gold, within and without. This ark also carries with it the thought of preservation. We see this when the children of Israel were crossing the Jordan. As the ark led the way, the children of Israel were preserved from the waters of the Jordan (death). The thought of preservation is seen in regard to the tables of the Law, the golden pot of manna, and Aaron's rod that budded, all of which were preserved in ark of the covenant.

The ark represents the throne of God on earth.

The ark represents the presence the God in Christ, by the spirit in the midst of His redeemed people.

The ark represents the glory of God, revealed in divine order and worship.

The ark represents the fullness of the Godhead, bodily revealed in the Lord Jesus Christ. All that the ark was to Israel in the Old Testament, Jesus Christ is to His church, spiritual Israel, in the New Testament. The ark of the covenant was placed in the holiest of all or the most holy place (holy of holies).

The materials of which the ark was composed represented His person; His work was the purpose for which it was used.

➢ What was inside the ark of the covenant? What did each represent?

The thought of preservation is seen in regard to the tables of the Law, the golden pot of manna, and Aaron's rod that budded, which were preserved in the ark of the covenant.

Tables of the Law are the tablets containing the Ten Commandments (Exodus 20; 31:18).

Golden pot of manna is bread from heaven. The people were to go out each day and gather enough for that day. In that way, God tested them to see whether they would follow His instructions. On the sixth day, they were to prepare what they brought in, and it was to be twice as much as they had gathered on the other days (Exodus 16:4).

Aaron's rod that budded was placed before the Lord in the tent of the covenant law. The next day, Moses entered the tent and saw that Aaron's staff, which represented the House of Levi, had not only sprouted but had budded, blossomed, and produced almonds. The Lord told Moses to put back Aaron's staff in front of the ark of the covenant law; it was to be kept as a sign to the rebellious to put an end to their grumbling against God so they would not die (Numbers 17:8, 10).

Worship in the Earthly Tabernacle

The first covenant had regulations for worship and an earthly sanctuary. A tabernacle was set up. In its first room were thee lampstands and the table, with its consecrated bread; this was called the holy place. Behind the second curtain was a room called the most holy place, which had the golden altar of incense and the gold-covered ark of the covenant. This ark contained the gold jar of of manna, Aaron's staff that had budded, and the stone tablets of the covenant. Above the ark were the cherubim of the glory, overshadowing the atonement cover (Hebrews 9:1–5).

The ark of the covenant measured 10 feet by 10 feet by 10 feet, or 1,000 feet cubic content. It was foursquare, as was the brazen altar, the golden altar, and the breastplate, or judgment, on the priest.

The Shekinah glory, the one who dwells. God's dwelling is visible among the people of God. His glory filled the four squares and covered the earth floor within the veil. The cubits point to the full glory of the kingdom, as set forth in the one thousand years spoken of in Revelation 20:1–6. The ultimate fulfillment and revelation is the glory of God in the new and heavenly Jerusalem, which is the foursquare and eternal city of God and the redeemed, according to Revelation 21.

Characteristics and Symbols of a Distinct Member of the Godhead

- The tables of the Law—a type of the Father, the Lawgiver. It was by His voice that the Law was first given. The Law is symbolic of all authority and power, which is in the hands of the Father.
- The golden pot of manna—In the Manna, we are directed to the Son of God, who is the bread of life and bread of heaven, which came down from above (John 6:48–45).
- Aaron's rod that budded—a type of God, the Holy Spirit, for in Aaron's rod, we see the principle of fruitfulness and life, as in Galatians 5:22–23.

Who Could Go into the Department of the Ark of the Covenant?

Christ is the mediator of a new covenant. Those who are called may receive the promised eternal inheritance, now that He has died, as a ransom to set them free from the sins committed under the first covenant. Christ did not enter a sanctuary made with human hands that was only a copy of the true one. He entered heaven itself, to appear for us in God's presence. He did not enter heaven to offer Himself again and again, the way the high priest enters the most holy place every year, with blood that is not His own. He would have had to suffer many times since the creation of the world. He has appeared, once for all, to do away with sin by the sacrifice of Himself (Hebrews 9:15, 24–26).

The tabernacle compared to the tabernacle that Jesus talked about when He made the statement, "Destroy this temple, and I will raise it again in three days" (John 2:19 NIV).

Jesus cleared the temple courts in Jerusalem because He found people selling cattle, sheep, and doves and found others sitting at tables, exchanging money. He made a whip out of cords and drove them all from the courts. The Jews asked Him, "What sign can you show us to prove your authority to do all this?"

Jesus answered, "Destroy this temple, and I will raise it again in three days." The temple He was speaking of was His body. He would be raised from the dead in three days. The disciples recalled what Jesus said and believed the scripture.

The divine purpose in the building of the tabernacle is God's desire to dwell in the midst of His redeemed people on His own terms and His own grounds.

God follows the pronouncement of His purpose by giving a pattern that is to be followed in the construction of His dwelling place. He said, "Let them make me a sanctuary; that I may dwell among them" (Exodus 25:8 KJV). He wanted them to know that He "I AM"—is the Lord, their God, who brought them out of Egypt (Exodus 29:46).

The believer needs to place value and emphasis where God does, and that concerns His dwelling place. God now dwells in the tabernacle, or dwelling place of the church. He dwells individually in each believer's heart. He also dwells corporately or collectively in the church as a body.

We have seen that God has dwelt with men, among men, and, finally, in men. Fellowship between God and man is necessary to fulfill God's purpose and plan in redemption.

Special Rules for the Priests

- A priest must not make himself ceremonially unclean for any of his people who die, except for a close relative—mother, father, son or daughter, brother, or unmarried sister dependent upon him. (Her having a husband may make him unclean.)
- He must not defile himself by people related to him by marriage.
- A priest must not shave his head or shave off the edges of his beard or cut his body.
- He must be holy to his God
- He must not profane the name of his God.
- He is to be holy because he presents the food offerings to the Lord. It's the food of his God.

This is how the high priest must enter the most holy place:

- He must first bring a young bull for a sin offering and a ram for a burnt offering.
- He must put on the sacred linen tunic, with undergarments next to his body.

- He must tie the linen sash around himself and put on the linen turban.
- He must bath himself with water before he puts on the sacred garments.
- He must take two male goats from the Israelite community for a sin offering and a ram for a burnt offering.
- The high priest must offer the bull for his own sin offering, to make atonement for himself and his household.
- He must take the two goats and present them before the Lord at the entrance to the tent of meeting.
- He must cast lots for the two goats—one lot for the Lord and the other for the scapegoat.
- The high priest must bring the goat whose lot falls to the Lord and sacrifice it for a sin offering.
- The scapegoat must be presented alive before the Lord to be used for making atonement by sending it into the wilderness.
- He must make atonement for the most holy place because of the uncleanness and rebellion of the Israelites, whatever their sins have been.

CHAPTER 4
The Tabernacle of David

The differences between the tabernacle of Moses and the tabernacle of David are as follows:

The tabernacle of Moses was moved to Gibeon during the Davidic era. The worship was moved also, and David set up a worship center in Zion. It was called a tent of meeting. It was also known as David's tabernacle. David instituted a nonsacrificial worship of praise and thanksgiving.

Zion was called the City of David when the tabernacle of David was pitched in Mount Zion. He placed a company of priests and Levites, who had been taken from the old order that they had known for years, as in Moses's tabernacle. These priests came into a new order, as pertaining to worship in David's tabernacle.

The tabernacle of David had no outer court with its attendant furniture and no holy place with its attendant furniture, in comparison to the tabernacle of Moses at Gibeon.

These priests and Levites simply had the holiest of all, or the most holy place, and in it was the ark of the covenant.

In comparison to the tabernacle of Moses and the priests at Mount Gibeon, these priests in the tabernacle at Zion did not offer animal sacrifices. They offered sacrifices of praise, joy, and thanksgiving. The ministry of the singers and musicians was in full operation. They were to offer up *spiritual sacrifice* in Mount Zion in the tabernacle of David.

Mary R. Winters, D. Min, Ph.D.

David appointed teams of worshippers who served in rotating shifts, day and night. Their duties consisted of praising the Lord with singing, prophesying, and playing musical instruments before the ark.

A number of psalms contain words spoken by the Lord. They came through various worshippers as they ministered under a prophetic anointing. Musical prophecy, both vocal and instrumental, was a feature of Davidic worship. David set apart some of the sons of Asaph for the ministry of prophesying. They were accompanied by harps, lyres, and cymbals.

In the Old Testament, David had transferred the ark of the covenant from the tabernacle of Moses to the tabernacle of David. There was simply a transference of the holiest of all. The priests in David's tabernacle could simply and boldly enter into the most holy place. They had access before the ark of the Lord. There was no standing veil between them and the ark, as there had been in the tabernacle of Moses. They had boldness to enter in within the veil because that veil belonged to the tabernacle of Moses, not to the tabernacle of David.

The sacrifices had been offered in dedication, and the animal sacrifices were no longer offered in David's tabernacle. It was only spiritual sacrifices. The purpose of David's tabernacle was to enhance the worship of God. It was to be a ministering priest unto the Lord in the priestly body of Christ.

> It is to be built into a spiritual house to be a holy priesthood, offering spiritual sacrifices acceptable to God through Jesus Christ. (1 Peter 2:5 NIV)

We discovered that there were two priesthoods ministering at the tabernacle at Gibeon and Zion. These were two priesthoods of the same Levitical tribe, yet each had their distinct functions. There were those priests who ministered at the tabernacle of Moses, and there were those priests who ministered at the tabernacle of David. A great contrast is seen in their respective functions. One priesthood functioned according to the Law and commandment of Moses; the other company functioned according to the commandment of David (Numbers 3:1–13; 1 Chronicles 16:38–40; 2 Chronicles l:l–3).[12]

Paul Bunty and David Collins[3]

> After this I will return, and will build again the tabernacle of David, which is fallen down; and I will build again the ruins thereof and I will set it up: That the residue

---

[1] Robert E. Webber, *The Complete Library of Christian Worship*, vol. 4 (City: Biblical Foundation of Christian Worship, year).

[2] Kevin J. Conner, *The Tabernacle of David* (City: City Bible Publishing, 1976).

[3] Paul Bunty and David Collins.

of men might seek after the Lord, and all the Gentiles, upon whom my name is called. (Acts 15:16–17 KJV; also see Amos 9:11–12)

Speaking to the gathering of the early church in Jerusalem, James said that the fact that the Gentiles were coming to the Lord was a result of the restoration of what David's tabernacle represented. The grace of God was a way open into the very holiest of all (see Hebrews 6:19; 8:1–2).

The tabernacle of David was a tent, just like the tabernacle of Moses, erected to serve as a place of worship. But while the tabernacle of Moses remained at Gibeon, with all the articles of furniture (except the ark of the covenant itself), the tabernacle of David was on Mount Zion. It had none of the other furniture, only the ark. Unlike Moses's tabernacle, it did not have three compartments—the outer court, the holy place, and the holiest of all (where the ark was supposed to be placed). It had only one compartment, the holiest of all. Yet people flowed in and out of David's tabernacle around the clock to worship before the Lord (2 Samuel 6:1–23; 1 Chronicles 13:1–14; 15:1;16:43).

The setting up of David's tabernacle and the events that led to it are highly significant for us; as James indicated in Acts 15:16–17, it prepictures the experience of the church. Just as David's tabernacle contained the ark of the covenant in open access to all Israel, so the church, through Christ, has open access to the presence of God and is the tabernacle that contains the glory of God (2 Corinthians 6:16; Ephesians 2:20–22).

Historical Background

The ark of the covenant had been removed from the tabernacle of Moses many years previously, when Israel was losing in a battle with the Philistines. They had brought the ark from the tabernacle into their midst, believing—superstitiously—that its presence would give them victory. However, they were miserably defeated, and the ark was taken captive into Philistine territory and put into the temple of Dagon. The Philistines, however, soon sent it back into the land of Israel because of the judgments that began to come upon them. It ended up in a house in the border town of Kiriath-Jearim and remained there for twenty years, until David became king of all Israel. Read the full account in 1 Samuel 4–7.

David's Great Desire

> David conferred with each of his officers, the commanders of thousands and commanders of hundreds. He said, to the whole assembly of Israel, if it seems good to you and if it is the will of the Lord our God, let us send word far and wide to the rest of our brothers throughout the territories of Israel and also to the priests and Levites who are with them in their towns and pasturelands, to come and join

us. Let us bring the ark of our God back to us, for we did not inquire of it during the reign of Saul. (1 Chronicles 13:1–3 KJV)

What Was the Ark?

For Israel, the ark was the presence of God in their midst. To them, it represented the throne of God.

> The Ark of God, the Lord, who is enthroned between the Cherubim. (1 Chronicles 13:6 KJV)

It meant that God was enthroned in their midst, ruling and reigning over the affairs of their lives.

The Name of God

> The Ark that is called by the Name. (1 Chronicles 13:6 NIV)

When Moses asked to know the name of the Lord, God answered.

> Moses said to God, "Suppose I go to the Israelites and say to them, 'The God of your fathers has sent me to you,' and they ask me, 'What is his name?' What shall I tell them?" God said to Moses, "I AM WHO I AM." This is what you are to say to the Israelites, "I AM has sent me to you." "...I am who I am." This is what you are to say to the Israelites: "I AM has sent me to you...This is my name forever, the name by which I am to be remembered from generation to generation" (Exodus 3:13–15 NIV)

That name *I AM* (Yahweh), sacred to Israel, represented all that God is! In the ark, all His power, authority, and righteous character was in their midst.

The Glory of God

"Above the ark were the cherubim of the Glory, overshadowing the place of atonement" (Hebrews 9:5 NIV; see also Exodus 25:10–22).

The fullness of God's glory was revealed in the ark. It was a "shadow" of what is in heaven (Hebrews 8:5; 10:1 NIV), where the "cherubim of the Glory" cover the throne, and the seraphim constantly call out to one another, "Holy, holy, holy is the Lord Almighty; the whole earth is full of his glory" (read Ezekiel 28:11–14; Isaiah 6:1–4).

To Israel, the ark meant

- communion with God (Exodus 25:22),
- direction and rest (Numbers 10:33–36),
- victory (Joshua 3; 4; 6), and
- revelation of His glory (Exodus 40:34–38; 2 Chronicles 5:2–14).

Three Items in the Ark

Behind the second curtain was a room called the Most Holy Place, which had … the gold-covered Ark of the Covenant. This Ark contained the Gold Jar of Manna, Aaron's Rod that had budded, and the Stone Tablets of the Covenant. (Hebrews 9:3–4 NIV)

Three things were inside the ark. Each depicted aspects of the Lord's nature:

- Aaron's rod (Numbers 17:5)—authority, anointing, fruitfulness
- Moses's tablets of stone (Exodus 25)—righteousness, holiness
- Pot of manna (Exodus 16:33–34; Luke 4:4)—sustenance of life, the living Word.

In understanding all that the ark meant to Israel, we understand David's great desire to bring it back into the midst of his people.

First Attempt—the Wrong Way

According to 2 Samuel 6:1–11 and 1 Chronicles 13, David's first attempt to bring back the ark was a failure. His plan was obviously to return it to Moses's tabernacle on Mount Gibeon, as he had not prepared anywhere else for it. He followed the same method as the Philistines when they sent it back to Israel and put it on a new cart, drawn by oxen. When Uzzah put his hand on the ark to steady it when the oxen stumbled, he was struck dead. David was angry (literally—"his nose is out of joint"). The ark was left in the house of a man called Obed-Edom and remained there for three months, bringing great blessing to all of his household.

Second Attempt—the Right Way

This time David found out from the Lord the right way to bring the ark back. Each truth also applies to the church:

- It had to be carried on the shoulders of a consecrated priesthood (1 Chronicles 15:2, 11–15). In the church, it is now the priesthood of all believers. The glory of the Lord will return in its fullness to a consecrated people. This consecration is expressed by the leaders first.
- It necessitated a new tent (the tabernacle of David) on a new mountain (Mount Zion) to house the ark (1 Chronicles 15:1). God was preparing His people as the place where He would reveal His glory.
- It required sacrifice (2 Samuel 6:13; 1 Chronicles 15:26; 16:1–2). The foundation of the church is always the sacrifice of Christ on the cross.

Wearing a linen ephod, David was dancing before the Lord with all his might, while he and all Israel were bringing up the ark of the Lord with shouts and the sound of trumpets. (2 Samuel 6:14–15 NIV)

The tabernacle of David was marked by the following:

- The presence of God is open to all. No "veil" barred the way into His presence, as it had in Moses's tabernacle (2 Corinthians 3:16–18).

Praise and worship twenty-four hours a day, with every musical instrument (Psalm 150.

- Songs in the spirit, coming with such spontaneity that a special ministry of a "recorder" was necessary; many of the psalms were written there.
- Unity—it was the experience of "all Israel."
- Great joy!

After this I will return and rebuild David's fallen tent. Its ruins I will rebuild and I will restore it, that the rest of mankind may seek the Lord, even all the Gentiles who bear my name, says the Lord (Acts 15:16–17 NIV)

CHAPTER 5
The Great Temples of Jerusalem

The Splendor of Solomon's Temple

The history of Solomon's temple reveals the spiritual condition of the nation and its kings, priests, and rulers. Its glory rises and falls under godly or ungodly leadership.

Over the years, the house of the Lord was plundered and desecrated by ungodly kings of Judah or Israel and Gentile kings. Under godly kings, there were great cleansings and fresh dedications of the temple services. The final days reveal the glory of the Lord departing from its holy oracle because of the great abominations that had been brought into it.

From the dedication of the temple under King Solomon in Jerusalem to its destruction and desolation under King Nebuchadnezzar of Babylon, we have a sad history.

> Unless the LORD builds the house, those who build it labor in vain. Unless the LORD watches over the city, the watchman stays awake in vain. It is in vain that you rise up early and go late to rest, eating the bread of anxious toil; for he gives to his beloved sleep. Behold, children are a heritage from the LORD, The fruit of the womb is a reward. Like arrows in the hand of a warrior, So are the children of

one's youth. Happy is the man who has his quiver full of them; They shall not be ashamed, But shall speak with their enemies in the gate. (Psalm 127:1–5 NKJV)

After the conquest of the land and the death of that great leader Joshua, the tribes of Israel settled into the chaotic, disjointed, and disorganized period described in the book of Judges. Nearly four centuries were characterized by the repeated descriptive phrase, "In those days there was no king in Israel, everyone did what was right in his own eyes" (Judges 21:25 KJV).

(Judges 17:6; 18:1; 19:1; 21:25 NIV) Failure to drive out and exterminate the corrupting Canaanites, who lived previously in the land, caused these people to grow back like poisonous weeds until they oppressed and harassed Israel. During this time, God graciously raised up "judges," who reversed the status quo for a season by calling on God and rallying the people around the one who had chosen them and commissioned them to occupy the land.

Moral and spiritual conditions were very low at Shiloh when the prophet Samuel was born. The Levitical priesthood under Eli was about to be disqualified in the deaths of Eli's disreputable sons, Hophni and Phinehas. Although God had desired to rule Israel as their invisible monarch and Lord, the people clamored for a national champion to rule them.

Then all the elders of Israel gathered together and came to Samuel at Ramah and said to him, "Behold, you are old and your sons do not walk in your ways; now appoint for us a king to govern us like all the nations." But the thing displeased Samuel when they said, "Give us a king to govern us." Samuel prayed to the LORD, and the LORD said to Samuel, "Hearken to the voice of the people in all that they say to you; for they have not rejected you, but they have rejected me from being king over them. According to all the deeds which they have done to me, from the day I brought them up out of Egypt, even to this day, forsaking me and serving other gods, so they are also doing to you. Now then, hearken to their voice, only you shall solemnly warn them, and show them the ways of the king who shall reign over them." So Samuel told all the words of the LORD to the people who were asking a king from him. He said, "These will be the ways of the king who will reign over you: he will take your sons and appoint them to his chariots and to be his horsemen, and to run before his chariots - and he will appoint for himself commanders of thousands and commanders of fifties, and some to plow his ground and to reap his harvest, and to make his implements of war and the equipment of his chariots." He will take your daughters to be perfumers and cooks and bakers. He will take the best of your fields and vineyards and olive orchards and give them to his servants. He will take the tenth of your grain and of your vineyards and give it to his officers and to his servants. He will take your menservants and maidservants, and the best of your cattle and your asses, and put them to his work. He will take the tenth of your flocks, and you shall be his slaves. And in that day you will cry out because of your king, whom you have chosen for yourselves; but the LORD will not answer you in that day." The people refused to listen to the voice of Samuel - and they said, "No, but we will have a king over us, that we also may be like all the nations, that our king may govern us and go out before us and fight our battles." And when Samuel had heard all the words of the people, he repeated them in the ears of the LORD. And the LORD said to Samuel, "Hearken to their voice, and make them a king. (1 Samuel 8:4–22 KJV)

The first king chosen, Saul, of the tribe of Benjamin, a son of Kish, though a man of proven military ability, failed the tests God gave him and was soon disqualified (1 Samuel 15), leaving the newly formed "monarchy" in a state of civil war. Young David, a Bethlehemite shepherd lad from the tribe of Judah, was then chosen by God. As everyone knows, he proved by his wise choices to be a man "after God's own heart." As a great military strategist David united the tribes and extended the national boundaries so that in his time, Israel enjoyed a greater fraction of the land promised to Abraham than has ever since been the case. David ruled as king for seven years in Hebron and then established his throne in Jerusalem after overcoming the ancient Jebusite (Canaanite) community there. His reign continued there in Jerusalem for the next thirty-two years. Secure on his throne and dwelling in a magnificent palace of cedar and stone, David began to concerned that he, the visible king, dwelled in a magnificent house, but the invisible King of kings still dwelt in an aging temporary tent, the tabernacle of Moses.

At first, the prophet Nathan gave David approval to construct a temple, but the following night, God intervened. Speaking to Nathan in a dream, God laid out for David an amazing covenant, whose promises continue to this present day. God committed himself to establishing the house of David forever, to a specific land and people (Israel), and to a temple, according to 2 Samuel 7. A Messiah, in fact, would be one of David's sons. David, a man of war, was not to build the first temple. That task was given to his son Solomon, although David drew up the plans. The fact that other nations had temples and Israel did not is not the reason the first temple was to be built. The temple was to be a memorial to Israel to turn her heart away from the idols of the surrounding nations. The temple would provide them an incentive not to practice the same evil things as the Canaanites. After the temple was built, the tabernacle was dismantled. It may have been stored in a room under the Temple Mount. It is quite possible it is still there to this day, as many rabbis and authorities in Jerusalem believe.

Mary R. Winters, D. Min, Ph.D.

No Perfect King

David was by no means a perfect king. He had a number of wives, and his marriages were apparently nothing to boast about. His grievous sin of murder and adultery in the case of Bathsheba brought war in David's household for the rest of his days. Yet when confronted with his sin, David showed contrition and repentance (Psalms 32; 51).

Late in his reign, David carelessly chose to take a census of the army, acting against the advice of General Joab and other army leaders. The Lord was provoked to great anger at David, who evidently had forgotten that the strength of Israel was in her God and not in the number of her soldiers or skill in battle. Confronted with the seriousness of his poor judgment by the prophet Gad, David was given three choices by God as to the consequences that were to follow this serious mistake on the part of the king. The three choices given him were (1) three years of famine, (2) three years of devastation by Israel's foes, or (3) three days of destruction (pestilence) wrought by the angel of the Lord (1 Chronicles 21; 2 Samuel 24). Knowing that God was merciful, David asked God to choose. The result was three terrible days of pestilence from the angel of the Lord. Jerusalem was spared at the last minute when David cried out for mercy—the sin was his and not that of the people; they were but sheep.

It was at this time, when the hand of the angel of the Lord was stayed, that David was told by Gad to erect an altar on the threshing floor of Araunah (Oman) the Jebusite. The location was on windswept Mount Moriah. The site is the place where, one thousand years earlier, God had stopped Abraham from sacrificing Isaac.

> And Gad came that day to David and said to him, "Go up, erect an altar to the Lord on the threshing floor of Araunah the Jebusite." … And David built there an altar unto the Lord, and offered burnt offerings and peace offerings. So the Lord heeded the prayers for the land, and the plague was withdrawn from Israel. (2 Samuel 24:15, 16–25 NKJV)

Plans and Preparations for the Temple

David's role and careful attention to all the details, plans, and preparation for the temple are recorded in 1 Chronicles 22. David commanded gather together the aliens who were in the land of Israel, and he set stonecutters to prepare dressed stones for building the house of God. David also provided great stores of iron for nails for the doors of the gates and for clamps, as well as bronze in quantities beyond weighing and cedar timbers without number, for the Sidonians and Tyrians brought great quantities of cedar to David.

David said, "Solomon my son is young and inexperienced, and the house that is to be built for the LORD must be exceedingly magnificent, of fame and glory throughout all lands; I will therefore make preparation for it." So David provided materials in great quantity before his death.

He called for Solomon his son, and charged him to build a house for the LORD, the God of Israel. David said to Solomon, "My son, I had it in my mind to build a house to the name of the LORD my God. But the word of the LORD came to me, saying, "you have shed much blood and have waged great wars; you shall not build a house to my name, because you have shed so much blood before me upon the earth. Behold, a son shall be born to you; he shall be a man of peace. I will give him peace from all his enemies round about; for his name shall be Solomon, and I -will give peace and quiet to Israel in his days. He shall build a house for my name. He shall be my son, and I will be his father, and I -will establish his royal throne in Israel forever."

Now, my son, the LORD be with you, so that you may succeed in building the house of the LORD your God, as he has spoken concerning you. Only, may the LORD grant you discretion and understanding, that when he gives you charge over Israel, you may keep the law of the LORD your God. Then you will prosper if you are careful to observe the statutes and the ordinances which the LORD commanded Moses for Israel. Be strong, and of good courage. Fear not, be not dismayed! With great pains, I have provided for the house of the LORD a hundred thousand talents of gold, a million talents of silver, and bronze and iron beyond weighing, for there is so much of it; timber and stone too, I have provided. To these you must add. You have an abundance of workmen: stonecutters, masons, carpenters, and all kinds of craftsmen without number, skilled in working gold, silver, bronze, and iron. Arise and be doing! The LORD be with you!"

David also commanded all the leaders of Israel to help Solomon his son, saying, "Is not the LORD your God with you? And has he not given you peace on every side? For he has delivered the inhabitants of the land into my hand and the land is subdued before the LORD and his people. Now set your heart and soul to seek the LORD your God. Arise and build the sanctuary of the LORD God, so that the Ark of the Covenant of the LORD and the holy articles of God may be brought into a house built for the name of the LORD." (1 Chronicles 22:5–19 NKJV)

Mary R. Winters, D. Min, Ph.D.

The Construction of the Temple

After the death of his father, David, Solomon issued the orders for the building of the first temple to commence:

> You know that my father David could not build a house for the name of the Lord his God because of the wars which were fought against him on every side until the Lord put his foes under the soles of his feet. (1 Kings 5:3 NIV)

The building of the first temple was a monumental task. Phoenician craftsmen were employed to build the temple. Construction began in the fourth year of Solomon's reign and took seven years:

Then, King Solomon raised up a labor force out of all Israel, and the labor force was thirty thousand men. Solomon selected 70,000 men to bear burdens, 80,000 to quarry stone in the mountains, and 3,600 to oversee them (1 Kings 5:13; 2 Chronicles 2:2 NIV).

The stones were hewn from a quarry and brought to the temple:

And the temple, when it was being built, was built with stone finished at the quarry, so that no hammer or chisel or any iron tool was heard in the temple while it was being built (1 Kings 6:7).

Generous sections of 1 Kings 5–8 and 2 Chronicles 1–7 give us great detail about the construction of the temple, the priesthood, and the temple services. A summary is given in 1 Kings 6:1–38:

> In the four hundred and eightieth year after the people of Israel came out of the land of Egypt, in the fourth year of Solomon's reign over Israel, in the month of Ziv, which is the second month, he began to build the house of the LORD. The house which King Solomon built for the LORD was sixty cubits long, twenty cubits wide, and thirty cubits high. The vestibule in front of the nave of the house was twenty cubits long, equal to the width of the house, and ten cubits deep in front of the house. And he made for the house windows with recessed frames. He also built a structure against the wall of the house, running round the walls of the house, both the nave the inner sanctuary and the side chambers all around. The lowest story was five cubits broad, the middle one was six cubits broad and the third was seven cubits broad, for around the outside of the house, he made offsets on the wall in order that the supporting beams should not be inserted into the walls of the house. When the house was built, it was with stone prepared at the quarry, so that neither hammer nor ax, nor any tool of iron was heard in the temple, while it was being built. The entrance for the lowest story was on the south side of the house and one went up by stairs to the middle story and from the middle story to the third. So he built the house, and finished it and he made the ceiling of the house of beams

and planks of cedar. He built the structure against the whole house, each story five cubits high, and it was joined to the house with timbers of cedar.

The word of the LORD came to Solomon, "Concerning this temple which you are building, if you walk in My statutes, execute My judgments, keep all My commandments and walk in them, then I will perform My word with you, which I spoke to your father David. I will dwell among the children of Israel, and will not forsake my people Israel."

So, Solomon built the house, and finished it. He lined the walls of the house on the inside with boards of cedar; from the floor of the house to the rafters of the ceiling, he covered them on the inside with wood and he covered the floor of the house with boards of cypress. He built twenty cubits of the rear of the house with boards of cedar from the floor to the rafters, and he built this within as an inner sanctuary, as the most Holy Place. The house, that is, the nave in front of the inner sanctuary, was forty cubits long. The cedar within the house was carved in the form of gourds and open flowers, all was cedar and no stone was seen. The inner sanctuary he prepared in the innermost part of the house, to set there, *the Ark of the Covenant* of the LORD. The inner sanctuary was twenty cubits long, twenty cubits wide, and twenty cubits high and he overlaid it with pure gold. He also made an altar of cedar.

Solomon overlaid the inside of the house with pure gold and he drew chains of gold across, in front of the inner sanctuary, and overlaid it with gold. He overlaid the whole house with gold until all the house was finished. Also the whole altar that belonged to the inner sanctuary he overlaid with gold. In the inner sanctuary he made two cherubim of olive wood, each ten cubits high, Five cubits were the length of one wing of the cherub, and five cubits the length of the other wing of the cherub; it was ten cubits from the tip of one wing to the tip of the other. The other cherub also measured ten cubits; both cherubim had the same measure and the same form. The height of one cherub was ten cubits and so was that of the other cherub. He put the cherubim in the innermost part of the house; and the wings of the cherubim were spread out so that a wing of one touched the one wall, and a wing of the other cherub touched the other wall. The other wings touched each other in the middle of the house. He overlaid the cherubim with gold. Solomon carved all the walls of the house round about with carved figures of cherubim and palm trees and open flowers, in the inner and outer rooms. The floor of the house he overlaid with gold in the inner and outer rooms. For the entrance to the inner sanctuary he made doors of olive wood; the lintel and the door posts formed a pentagon. He covered the two doors of olive wood with carvings of cherubim, palm trees, and open flowers; he overlaid them with gold, and spread gold upon the cherubim and upon the palm trees. He also made for the entrance, to the nave door posts, of olive wood, in the form of a square, and two doors of cypress wood; the two leaves of the one door were folding, and the two leaves of the other door were folding. On them he carved cherubim and palm trees and open flowers; and he overlaid them with gold evenly applied upon the carved work. He built the inner court with three courses of hewn stone and one course of cedar beams. In the fourth year the foundation of the house of the LORD was laid, in the month of Ziv and in the eleventh year, in the month of Bui, which is the eighth month, the house was finished in all its parts, and according to all its specifications. He was seven years in building it.[4]

Dedication

After the completion of the temple, it was dedicated by King Solomon in 953 BC. Solomon's speech to the people and his marvelous prayers were followed by an enormous offering of 22,000 oxen and 120,000 sheep. A great public feast followed:

> Solomon held the feast at that time; and all Israel with him, a great assembly, from the entrance of Hamath to the Brook of Egypt; before the LORD our God, seven days. On the eighth day, he sent the people away and they blessed the king and went to their homes, joyful and glad of heart for all the goodness that the LORD had shown to David his servant and to Israel his people. (1 Kings 8:65–66 KJV)

> When Solomon had ended his prayer, fire came down from heaven and consumed the burnt offering and the sacrifices, and the glory of the LORD filled the temple. The priests could not enter the house of the LORD, because the glory of the LORD filled the LORD'S house. When all the children of Israel saw the fire come down and the glory of the LORD upon the temple, they bowed down with their faces to the earth on the pavement, and worshiped and gave thanks to the LORD saying, *"For he is good, for his steadfast love endures far ever."* Then the king and all the people offered sacrifice before the LORD. King Solomon offered as a sacrifice twenty-two thousand oxen and a hundred and twenty thousand sheep.

---

[4] Kevin J. Connor, *The Temple of Solomon* (City Bible Publishing).

So the king and all the people dedicated the house of God. The priests stood at their posts, the Levites also, with the instruments for music to the LORD which King David had made for giving thanks to the LORD for his steadfast love. Love endures forever whenever David offered praises by their ministry, opposite them the priests sounded trumpets; and all Israel stood. (2 Chronicles 7:1–6 NIV)

A Temple without an Idol

The feature that set apart the Solomonic temple from other temples in the ancient world is that there was no idol in it. It contained only the mercy seat over the ark and the cherubim overshadowing the mercy seat. This declared to the world that idols were unnecessary for God to be present. The God of Israel was not localized in any sense. Neither was He bound to any other form, such as the ark. The temple, therefore, was not necessary because of God's nature. He did not need it. One thousand years later, the first Christian martyr, Stephen, said to an unruly crowd:

Solomon built God a house. However, the Most High does not dwell in temples made with hands, as the prophet says: "Heaven is My throne, and the earth is my footstool. What house will you build for Me, says the Lord or what is the place of My rest? Has My hand not made all these things?" (Acts 7:47–50, quoting Isaiah 66:1–2 NKJV)

The temple was built to meet the limitations and needs of God's people. It emphasized the way of salvation to those who asked His forgiveness and represented the believers' assurance of the grace of God for their joy and blessing (1 Kings 8:27–30).

But will God indeed dwell on the earth? Behold, heaven and the highest heaven cannot contain thee; how much less this house which I have built! (1 Kings 8:27)

The temple also symbolized the hearing ear of God.

Yet regard the prayer of Your servant and his supplication, O Lord my God, and listen to the cry and the prayer which Your servant is praying before You today: that Your eyes may be open toward this temple night and day toward the place of which You said, "My name shall be there" and that You may hear the prayer which Your servant makes toward this place. (1 Kings 8:28–29 NKJV)

It was also a place of refuge for the stranger.

> Moreover concerning a foreigner, who is not of Your people Israel, but has come from a far country for Your name's sake, (for they will hear of Your great name and Your strong hand and Your outstretched arm), when he comes and prays toward this temple, hear in heaven Your dwelling place, and do according to all for which the foreigner calls to You, that all peoples of the earth may know Your name and fear You, as do Your people Israel, and that they may know that this temple which I have built is called by your name. (1 Kings 8:41–43 NKJV)

The temple is the house of prayer for all people, where all nations of the earth should fear God.

> Even them I will bring to My holy mountain, and make them joyful in My House of prayer. Their burnt offerings and their sacrifices will be accepted on My altar; for My house shall be called a house of prayer for all nations. (Isaiah 56:7 NKJV)

Fading Splendor—The Temple of Solomon

Solomon's great wisdom and the unrivaled splendor of the first temple brought pilgrims from near and far. The account of the visit of the Queen of Sheba tells us something about this great king and the magnificent and holy light from God that blessed him and all the people. Solomon failed to heed the counsel of God and of his father, David. He soon had accumulated horses and chariots (disregarding the admonition of Samuel and the Law of Moses), and in the course of time he excelled his father's love of women by accumulating "700 wives and 300 concubines." One of the great understatements of the Bible attributes Solomon's downfall to the influence of his foreign wives.

> Now King Solomon loved many foreign women (2 Chronicles 9; 1 Kings 10 NKJV) the daughter of Pharaoh, and Moabite, Ammonite, Edomite, Sidonian, and Hittite women, from the nations concerning which the LORD had said to the people of Israel, "You shall not enter into marriage with them, neither shall they with you, for surely they will turn away your heart after their gods; Solomon clung to these in love. He had seven hundred wives, princesses, and three hundred concubines; and his wives turned away his heart. When Solomon was old his wives turned away his heart after other gods and his heart was not wholly true to the LORD his God, as was the heart of David his father. Solomon went after Ashtoreth the goddess of the Sidonians, and after Milcom the abomination of the Ammonites. Solomon did what was evil in the sight of the LORD, and did not wholly follow the LORD, as David his father had done. Then Solomon built a high place for Chemosh the

abomination of Moab, and for Molech the abomination of the Ammonites, on the mountain east of Jerusalem. And so he did for all his foreign wives, who burned incense and sacrificed to their gods. And the LORD was angry with Solomon, because his heart had turned away from the LORD, the God of Israel, who had appeared to him twice, and had commanded him concerning this thing, that he should not go after other gods; but he did not keep what the LORD commanded. Therefore; the LORD said to Solomon, "Since this has been your mind and you have not kept my covenant and my statutes which I have commanded you, I will surely tear the kingdom from you and will give it to your servant. Yet, for the sake of David your father, I will not do it in your days but, I will tear it out of the hand of your son. However, I will not tear away all the Kingdoms; but, I will give one tribe to your son, for the sake of David my servant and for the sake of Jerusalem which I have chosen." (1 Kings 11:1–13 NIV)[5]

For many years, Solomon evidently wandered away from fellowship with his God, returning only much later, near the end of his life, to record for us in his book, Ecclesiastes, what he had learned about the emptiness of all of life apart from God. When Solomon died, his son Rehoboam became king of Israel. The nation, however, was in a spiritual decline. Rehoboam's policies caused the kingdom to be divided into north (Israel) and south (Judah), separate regimes. Jeroboam, the first king of Israel, built two substitute places of worship, one in Bethel and one in Dan, for fear the people would return to Jerusalem:

And Jeroboam said in his heart, "Now the kingdom may return to the house of David. If these people go up to offer sacrifices in the house of the Lord at Jerusalem, then the heart of this people will turn back to their lord, Rehoboam king of Judah, and they will kill me and go back to Rehoboam king of Judah." Therefore the king took counsel and made two calves of gold and said to the people. "It is too much for you to go up to Jerusalem. Here are your gods, O Israel, which brought you up from the land of Egypt." (1 Kings 12:26–28 NKJV)

Because the people felt bound to the legal system of worship in Jerusalem, Jeroboam realized the need that worship be centralized in the north. The Northern Kingdom remained in idolatry until it was overrun and taken captive in 721 BC by the Assyrians. Nineteen kings had ruled over the ten northern tribes—the Bible has no good thing to say about a single one of them. The dismal record of the lives of Jeroboam I, Nadab, Baasha, Elah, Zimri, Omri, Ahab, Ahaziah, Jehoram

---

[5] *The Layman's Parallel Bible, New International Version* (The Zondervan Corporation, 1991).

(Joram), Jehu, Jehoahaz, Jehoash (Joash), Jeroboam II, Zechariah, Shallum, Menahem, Pekahiah, Pekah, and Hoshea is given in the books of the Kings.[25]

Zerubbabel's Temple

The second temple was called Zerubbabel's temple. Cyrus, king of Persia, authorized the return of the Jewish captives, the return of the temple vessels Nebuchadnezzar had looted. The reconstruction of the temple (about 537 BC) was finished about 515 BC The completed temple was smaller than and more inferior to Solomon's temple. The ark of the covenant was never recovered, and so the second temple (and Herod's temple) had no ark.

There are many stories as to where the ark is today. Some claim that it is under the Temple Mount and has been seen by rabbis. Others claim that when Solomon's temple was looted in 1 Kings 14:26 that the Egyptian king also took the ark and placed it within a replica of the temple itself in Egypt. Some even claim that Solomon gave the Queen of Sheba the ark as a present and that it sits in Ethiopia today. More than likely, this ark in Ethiopia is just a replica of the actual ark. Solomon's ten lampstands were not recovered either. One seven-branched candelabrum, the table of showbread and the altar of incense stood in the holy place of the second temple (as they did in Herod's temple). These were taken by Antiochus IV Epiphanes (about 175–163 BC), who defiled the altar in 167 BC. The Maccabees cleansed the temple, restored its furnishings in 164 BC (1 Macc. 4:36–59), and later turned it into a fortress.[6]

In the subsequent history of the Israelite people, we see that God's anger and punishment fell on them because they were unfaithful to the conditions of the covenant. They did not give heed to the exhortations of the prophets or their warnings. The Israelite nation received from God the consequences of their sin.

Second Kings 25 describes this vividly. All the warnings of the prophets were fulfilled word for word. The able-bodied people who remained in the city were taken as slaves to Babylon.

In the fourteenth year after the destruction of the city, the prophet Ezekiel was given a vision regarding the reconstruction of the temple.

> In the twenty-fifth year of our exile, at the beginning of the year, on the tenth of the month, in the fourteenth year after the fall of the city, on that very day the hand of the Lord was on me and he took me there. In visions of God he took me to the land of Israel and set me on a very high mountain, on whose south side were some buildings that looked like a city. He took me there, and I saw a man whose appearance was like bronze; he was standing in the gateway with a linen cord and

---

[6] The Second Temple, Zerubbabel's Temple, "Desecrated and ransacked, but not destroyed and torn down." http://www.endtimeinfo.net/temple/whichtemple.html.

a measuring rod in his hand. The man said to me, "Son of man, look carefully and listen closely and pay attention to everything I am going to show you, for that is why you have been brought here. Tell the people of Israel everything you see. I saw a wall completely surrounding the temple area. The length of the measuring rod in the man's hand was six long cubits, each of which was a cubit and a handbreadth. He measured the wall; it was one measuring rod thick and one rod high. (Ezekiel 40:1–5 NIV)

In 536 BC, the Persian king Cyrus conquered Babylon. He permitted the Israelites to return to Jerusalem and rebuild temple. He also gave them back the precious things, gold, and silver that Nebuchadnezzar had looted from the temple and brought to Babylon. The Israelites who returned under the leadership of Zerubbabel began the reconstruction of the temple. The work was completed in 515, but the people lamented that it could not stand comparison with Solomon's temple.

The renovated temple became the center of the religious observances, rituals of worship, and festival celebrations. The state of affairs continued to exist until, in 33 BC, Alexander the Great conquered Palestine and brought the Israelites under Greek rule. The Greek rulers maintained respect and reverence toward the temple of Jerusalem and its liturgical regulations. But King Antiochus Epiphanes IV, king of the Seleucid Empire, unleashed persecution against the Jews. He consecrated the temple to the gods. He brought vogue activities into it that desecrated the sanctity of the temple and banned their religious observances. It was in response to all this that the Maccabees' rebellion and the purification of the temple took place. All this history is recorded in the first and second book of the Maccabees.

According to the book of Haggai, the people had returned from exile and had lived in Jerusalem for some years, but the temple still lay in ruins. The messages from the Lord urged the leaders of the people to rebuild the temple, and the Lord promised prosperity and peace in the future for a renewed and purified people.

And again the word of the Lord came unto Haggai in the four and twentieth day of the months saying, Speak to Zerubbabel, governor of Judah, saying, I will shake the heavens and the earth; And I will overthrow the throne of kingdoms, and I will destroy the strength of the kingdoms of the heathen; and I will overthrow the chariots, and those that ride in them; and the horses and their riders shall come down, everyone by the sword of his brother. In that day, saith the Lord of hosts, will I take thee, O Zerubbabel, my servant, the son of Shealtiel, saith the Lord, and will make thee as a signet: for I have chosen thee saith the Lord of hosts. (Haggai 2:20–23 KJV)

This is a reminder relating to the overthrow of earthly kingdoms. Man's buildings collapse before his eyes. So it is with our sovereign God, who will shake, overturn, shatter, and overthrow. In the midst of all this, God's covenant will be preserved, so that His eternal purposes will be fulfilled. Not only is it the protective hand of God but His glorious redemptive work.

Those who look to the world for a lasting kingdom must eventually be disappointed because the best things of this world must disappear.

Zerubbabel's descendant King Jehoiachin had been rejected by God, and a curse was pronounced upon him and his offspring (Jeremiah 22:30). The Lord said to his grandson Zerubbabel, "I will make you like a signet ring." God is at work! Because of Zerubbabel's faithfulness, the curse on his family has been lifted. The signet ring is back on God's finger. God was reversing His judgment, renewing His promise that the Davidic line would not die, but would one day give the world a Savior (Matthew 1:12; Luke 3:27). Zerubbabel himself never sat on the throne, but one of his descendants did.[7]

> And after they were brought to Babylon, Jechonias begat Salathiel; and Salathiel begat Zorobabel; And Zorobabel begat Abiud; and Abiud begat Eliakim; and Eliakim begat Azor; And Azor begat Sadoc; and Sadoc begat Achim; and Achim begat Eliud; And Eliud begat Eleazar; and Eleazar begat Matthan; and Matthan begat Jacob; And Jacob begat Joseph the husband of Mary, of whom was born Jesus, who is called Christ So all the generations from Abraham to David are fourteen generations; and from David until the carrying away into Babylon are fourteen generations; and from the carrying away into Babylon unto Christ are fourteen generations. (Matthew 1:12–17 KJV)

Herod's Temple/Christ Time

The Gospels of Matthew, Mark, and Luke mentioned words that were uttered by Jesus as He stood looking at the temple that reared its head like a caste mark on the brow of the holy city of Jerusalem. This magnificent temple was built on the mountaintop with incomparable grandeur, glory, beauty, and charm. Jesus's words indicated the destruction that was about to befall the city and the temple. The picture of the history of the Jewish temple of Jerusalem presents, on the one hand, great glory and eminence but punishment and destruction on the other. In AD 70 occurred a total destruction of this sacred building, believed to be filled with God's presence and glory. For all these twenty centuries, it has not been possible to reconstruct it. Even today, pilgrims visiting the city of Jerusalem can witness the lamentation over its demolition and the keen thirst and urgent

---

[7] Dr. Vincent Leoh, "Fulfilling God's Destiny for Your Life." April 2001.

prayer for its reconstruction, arising from the stones of the wall to the south of the specious grounds where the temple was once situated. We get an idea of their great expectations, until now unrealized.

The destruction of the city and the temple of Jerusalem were a turning point in the history of the Jewish people. The story of their exile, starting from those days and extending over the last twenty centuries, has been a tale of pain and woe. Though several countries tried to wipe them away from the face of the earth, no one has succeeded in totally eliminating them. Relief from the sufferings and exile of a nation that God had chosen as his own, to a certain extent, came only with the establishment of the state of Israel in 1948. Are we not witnesses to the fact of history that whatever they lost is being restored to them one by one by God? "I give this land to you and your descendants¹ God had promised Abraham. Accordingly, God had given this land to the Israelite nation. Though the land was lost to them in AD 70, it is now theirs, and they have recaptured the holy city of Jerusalem and made it their own. There is only one thing that remains without being reconstructed: the temple of Jerusalem. Is its reconstruction possible? If so, when? Where? How? These questions remain unanswered in the minds of several people.

The temple of Jerusalem is closely connected with the life of Jesus. The infant Jesus was presented in this temple. Mary and Joseph found the boy Jesus, who was lost for three days, here in this temple.

> And when the days of her purification according to the law of Moses were accomplished, they brought him to Jerusalem, to present him to the Lord; (As it is written in the law of the Lord, Every male that openeth the womb shall be called holy to the Lord;) And to offer a sacrifice according to that which is said in the law of the Lord, A pair of turtledoves, or two young pigeons. And, behold, there was a man in Jerusalem, whose name was Simeon; and the same man was just and devout, waiting for the consolation of Israel: and the Holy Ghost was upon him. And it was revealed unto him by the Holy Ghost, that he should not see death, before he had seen the Lord's Christ And he came by the Spirit into the temple: and when the parents brought in the child Jesus, to do for him after the custom of the law, Then took he him up in his arms, and blessed God, and said, Lord, now lettest thou thy servant depart in peace, according to thy word: For mine eyes have seen thy salvation, Which thou hast prepared before the face of all people; A light to lighten the Gentiles, and the glory of thy people Israel. And Joseph and his mother marvelled at those things which were spoken of him. And Simeon blessed them, and said unto Mary his mother, Behold, this child is set for the fall and rising again of many in Israel; and for a sign which shall be spoken against; (Yea, a sword shall pierce through thy own soul also,) that the thoughts of many hearts may be revealed. (Luke 2:22–35 KJV)

Now his parents went to Jerusalem every year at the feast of the passover. And when he was twelve years old, they went up to Jerusalem after the custom of the feast And when they had fulfilled the days, as they returned, the child Jesus tarried behind in Jerusalem; and Joseph and his mother knew not of it. But they, supposing him to have been in the company, went a day's journey; and they sought him among their kinsfolk and acquaintance, And when they found him not, they turned back again to Jerusalem, seeking him. And it came to pass, that after three days they found him in the temple, sitting in the midst of the doctors, both hearing them, and asking them questions. And all that heard him were astonished at his understanding and angers. And when they saw him, they were amazed: and his mother said unto him, Son, why hast thou thus dealt with us? behold, thy father and I have sought thee sorrowing. And he said unto them, How is it that ye sought me? wist ye not that I must be about my Father's business? And they understood not the saying which he spake unto them. And he went down with them, and came to Nazareth, and was subject unto them: but his mother kept all these sayings in her heart, And Jesus increased in wisdom and stature, and in favour with God and man. (Luke 2:41–52 KJV)

Jesus refers to the temple as the "House of God," "My father's house," and "My house shall be called a house of prayer for all the nations."

How he entered into the house of God, and did eat the shewbread, which was not lawful for him to eat, neither for them which were with him, but only for the priests? (Matthew 12:4 KJV)

And said unto them that sold doves, Take these things hence; make not my Father's house a house of merchandise. (John 2:16 KJV)

And he taught, saying unto them, Is it not written, My house shall be called of all nations the house of prayer? But ye have made it a den of thieves. (Mark 11:17 KJV)

He reproved very severely those who desecrated the temple with commercial activities. He told Peter how to procure the money to pay the temple tax, though he was not obliged to do so. Jesus took part in the prayer services and the sacrifices offered in the temple. He sat in the temple, taught the disciples, and healed several sick people. He came to the temple for every festival. Jesus's life was closely associated with the temple.

Today, we cannot see a single stone upon a stone. In the course of time, Muslims captured the place and built a splendid mosque instead of the temple. The Muslims consider it as their most sacred house of worship because they associate Muhamad Nabi with the city of Jerusalem.

The destruction of the temple still continues as a big loss for the Jews.[8]

---

[8] Joseph Kappil, *Through the Homeland of Jesus,* "The Rise and Fall of Temple of Jerusalem." http://www. Datanumeric.com/vlm/10-98/23.html.

CHAPTER 6

The 400 Years between the Old and New Testaments

by Ray C. Stedman

At the close of the book of Malachi in the Old Testament, the nation of Israel is back again in the land of Palestine after the Babylonian captivity, but they are under the domination of the great world power of that day, Persia and the Medio-Persian empire. In Jerusalem, the temple had been restored, although it was a much smaller building than the one that Solomon had built and decorated in such marvelous glory.

Within the temple the line of Aaronic priests was still worshipping and carrying on the sacred rites as they had been ordered to do by the Law of Moses. There was a direct line of descendancy in the priesthood that could be traced back to Aaron.

But the royal line of David had fallen on evil days. The people knew who the rightful successor to David was and in the book of Haggai, Zechariah and Malachi, his name is given to us. It was Zerubbabel, the royal prince, yet there was no king on the throne of Israel, they were a puppet nation, under the domination of Persia. Nevertheless, although they were beset with weakness and formalism as the prophets have shown us, the people were united. There were no political schisms or factions among them, nor were they divided into groups or parties.

Now when you open the New Testament to the book of Matthew, you discover an entirely different atmosphere; almost a different world. Rome is now the dominant power of the earth. The Roman legions have spread throughout the length and breadth of the civilized world. The center of power has shifted from the East to the West, to Rome. Palestine is still a puppet state, the Jews never did regain their own sovereignty, but now there is a king on the throne. But this king is the descendant of Esau instead of Jacob, and his name is Herod the Great. Furthermore, the high priests who now sit in the seat of religious authority in the nation are no longer from the line of Aaron. They cannot trace their descendancy back, rather, they are hired priests to whom the office is sold as political patronage.

The temple is still the center of Jewish worship, although the building has been partially destroyed and rebuilt about a half-dozen times since the close of the Old Testament. But, now the synagogues that have sprung up in every Jewish city seem to be the center of Jewish life even more than the temple.

At this time, the people of Israel were split into three major parties. Two of them, the Pharisees and Sadducees, were much more prominent than the third. The smaller group, the Essenes, could hardly be designated as a party. Not long ago, however, they came into great prominence in our time and took on new significance because they had stowed away some documents in caves overlooking the Dead Sea. These documents were brought to light again by the accidental discovery of an Arab shepherd boy and are known as the Dead Sea Scrolls.

Now, what happened in these four hundred so-called "silent" years after the last of the inspired prophets spoke and the first of the New Testament writers began to write? You remember there is a word in Paul's letter to the Galatians that says, "But when the time had fully come, God sent forth his Son, born of woman, born under the law." (Gal. 4:4 NIV) In other words, the time of our Lord's birth was God's appointed hour, the moment for which God had been long preparing. Some of the exciting preparations took place during that time of "silence," however; you will understand your New Testament much better if you understand something of the historic events during the time between the Testaments.

After Malachi had ceased his prophesying and the canon of the Old Testament closed; the number of the books in the Old Testament was fulfilled and the inspired prophets ceased to speak. God allowed a period of time for the teachings of the Old Testament to penetrate throughout the world. During this time, He rearranged the scenes of history, much as a stage crew will rearrange the stage sets after the curtain has fallen and when the curtain rises again, there is an entirely new setting.

In about 435 B.C., when the prophet Malachi ceased his writing, the center of world power began to shift from the East to the West. Up to this time, Babylon had been the major world power, but, this was soon succeeded by the Medio-Persian Empire, as you remember from ancient history. This shift had been predicted by the Prophet Daniel, who said that there would rise up a bear who was higher on one side, than the other, signifying the division between Media and Persia, with the Persians the predominant ones. "And there before me was a second beast, which looked like a bear. It was raised up on one of its sides, and it had three ribs in its mouth between its teeth. It was told, Get up and eat your fill of flesh!" (Dan. 7:5 NIV).

At the height of the Persian power there arose in the country of Macedonia (which we now know as Greece), north of the Black Sea, a man by the name of Philip of Macedon, who became a leader in his own country. He united the islands of Greece and became their ruler. His son was destined to become one of the great world leaders of all time, Alexander the Great. In 330 B.C. a tremendous battle between the Persians and the Greeks entirely altered the course of history. In that battle, Alexander, as a young man only twenty years old, led the armies of Greece in victory over the Persians and completely demolished the power of Persia. The center of world power then shifted farther west into Greece and the Grecian empire was born.

A year after that historic battle, Alexander the Great led his armies down into the Syrian world toward Egypt. On the way, he planned to lay siege to the city of Jerusalem. As the victorious armies of the Greeks approached the city, word was brought to the Jews in Jerusalem that the armies were on their way. The high priest at that time, who was a godly old man by the name of Jaddua (who, by the way, is mentioned in the Bible in the book of Nehemiah) took the sacred writings of Daniel the prophet and accompanied by a host of other priests, dressed in white garments, went forth and met Alexander some distance outside the city. All this is from the report of Josephus, the Jewish historian, who tells us that Alexander left his army and hurried to meet this body of priests. When he met them, he told the high priest that he had a vision the night before, in which God had shown him an old man, robed in a white garment, who would show him something of great significance to himself, according to the account, the high priest then opened the prophecies of Daniel and read them to Alexander.

In the prophecies Alexander was able to see the predictions that he would become that notable goat with the horn in his forehead who would come from the West and smash the power of Medio-Persia and conquer the world. He was so overwhelmed by the accuracy of this prophecy and by the fact that it spoke about him, that he promised that he would save Jerusalem from siege and sent the high priest back with honors. How true is that account? It is very difficult at this distance in time to say, that at any event, this is the story.

Alexander died in 323 B.C. when he was only about thirty-three years old. He had drunk himself to death in the prime of his life, grieved because he had no more worlds to conquer. After his death, his empire was torn with dissension, because he had left no heir. His son had been murdered earlier, so there was no one to inherit the empire of Alexander.

After some time, however; the four generals that had led Alexander's armies divided his empire between them. Two of them are particularly noteworthy to us, one was Ptolemy, who gained Egypt and the northern African countries; the other was Seleucus, who gained Syria, to the north of Palestine. During this time Palestine was annexed by Egypt and suffered greatly athe hands of Ptolemy. In fact, for the next one hundred years, Palestine was caught in the meat grinder of the unending conflicts between Syria on the north and Egypt on the south.

Now, if you have read the prophecies of Daniel, you will recall that Daniel was able, by inspiration, to give a very accurate and detailed account of the highlights of these years of conflict between the king of the North (Syria) and the king of the South (Egypt). The eleventh chapter of Daniel gives us a most amazingly accurate account of that which has long since been fulfilled. If you want to see just how accurate the prophecy is, I suggest you compare that chapter of Daniel with the historical record of what actually occurred during that time. H. A. Ironside's little Book, *The 400 Silent Years,* gathers that up in some detail.

During this time Grecian influence was becoming strong in Palestine. A party arose among the Jews called the Hellenists, who were very eager to bring Grecian culture and thought into the nation and to liberalize some of the Jewish laws. This forced a split into two major parties. There were those who were strong Hebrew nationalist, who wanted to preserve everything according to the Mosaic order. They resisted all the foreign influences that were coming in to disrupt the old Jewish ways. This party became known as the Pharisees, which means "to separate." They were the separationists who insisted on preserving traditions. They grew stronger and stronger, becoming more legalistic and rigid in their requirements until they became the target for some of the most scorching words our Lord ever spoke. They had become religious hypocrites, keeping the outward form of the law, but, completely violating its spirit. On the other hand, the Hellenists; the Greek lovers, became more and more influential in the politics of the land. They formed the party that was known in New Testament days as the Sadducees, the liberals. They turned away from the strict interpretation of the law and became the rationalists of their day, ceasing to believe in the supernatural in any way. We are told in the New Testament that they came again and again to the Lord with questions about the supernatural, like "What will happen to a woman who has been married to seven different men? In the resurrection, whose wife will she be?" (Matt. 22:23-33 NKJV) They did not believe in a resurrection, but in these questions they were trying to put Jesus on the spot.

Now, there was also a young rebel Jewish priest who married a Samaritan, went down to Samaria, and in rebellion against the Jewish laws, built a temple on Mount Gerizim that became a rival of the temple in Jerusalem, This caused intense, fanatical rivalry between the Jews and the Samaritans and this rivalry is also reflected in the New Testament.

Also during this time, in Egypt, under the reign of one of the Ptolemies, the Hebrew scriptures were translated for the first time into another language, in about 284 B.C. A group of 70 scholars was called together by the Egyptian king to make a translation of the Hebrew Scriptures. Book by book they translated the Old Testament into Greek. When they had finished, it was given the name of the Septuagint, which means 70, because of the number of translators. This became the Greek version of the Hebrew Bible. From it, many of the quotations in the New Testament are derived. That is why New Testament quotations of Old Testament verses are sometimes in different words because they come from the Greek translation. The Septuagint is still in existence today and is widely used in various parts of the world. It is still a very important document.

A little later on, about 203 B.C., a king named Antiochus the Great came into power in Syria, to the north of Palestine. He captured Jerusalem from the Egyptians and began the reign of Syrian power over Palestine. He had two sons, one of whom succeeded him and reigned only a few years. When he died, his brother took the throne. This man, named Antiochus Epiphanes, became one of the most vicious and violent persecutors of the Jews ever known. In fact, he is often called the Antichrist of the Old Testament, since he fulfills some of the predictions of Daniel concerning the coming of one who would be "a contemptible person" and "a vile king." His name (which he modestly bestowed upon himself) means "Antiochus the Illustrious." Nevertheless, some of his own courtiers evidently agreed more with the prophecies of Daniel, and they changed two letters in his title from Epiphanes to Epipames, which means "the mad man."

His first act was to depose the high priest in Jerusalem thus ending the long line of succession, beginning with Aaron and his sons through the many centuries of Jewish life. Onias the Third was the last of the hereditary line of priests. Antiochus Epiphanes sold the priesthood to Jason, who was not of the priestly line. Jason, in turn, was tricked by his younger brother Menelaus, who purchased the priesthood and then sold the golden vessels of the temple in order to make up the tribute money. Epiphanes overthrew the God-authorized line of priests. Then, and under his reign, the city of Jerusalem and all the religious rites of the Jews began to deteriorate as they came fully under the power of the Syrian king.

In 171 B.C. Antiochus invaded Egypt and once again Palestine was caught in the nutcracker of rivalry. Palestine is the most fought over country in the world and Jerusalem is the most captured city in all history. It has been pillaged, ravished, burned and destroyed more than 27 times in its history.

While Antiochus was in Egypt, it was reported that he had been killed in battle and Jerusalem rejoiced. The people organized a revolt and overthrew Menelaus, the pseudo-priest. When report reached Antiochus (who was very much alive in Egypt) that Jerusalem was delighted at the report of his death, he organized his armies and swept like a fury back across the land, falling upon Jerusalem with terrible vengeance.

He overturned the city, regained his power and guided by the treacherous Menelaus, intruded into the very Holy of Holies. In the temple itself, some 40,000 people were slain in three days of fighting during this terrible time. When he forced his way into the Holy of Holies, he destroyed the scrolls of the law and, to the absolute horror of the Jews, took a sow and offered it upon the sacred altar. Then with a broth made from the flesh of this unclean animal, he sprinkled everything in the temple, thus completely defiling and violating the sanctuary. It is impossible for us to grasp how horrifying this was to the Jews. They were simply appalled that anything like this could ever happen to their sacred temple.

It was that act of defiling the temple which is referred to by the Lord Jesus as the "desolating sacrilege" which Daniel had predicted (Matt. 24:15 NKJV), which also became a sign of the coming desolation of the temple when the Antichrist himself will enter the temple, call himself God and thus defile the temple in that time. As we know from the New Testament, that still lies in the future.

Daniel the prophet had said the sanctuary would be polluted for 2300 days. (Dan. 8:14 NKJV) In exact accordance with that prophecy, it was exactly 2300 days, six and a half years, before the temple was cleansed. It was cleansed under the leadership of a man now famous in Jewish history, Judas Maccabaeus. He was one of the priestly lines who, with his father and four brothers, rose up in revolt against the Syrian king. They captured the attention of the Israelites, summoned them to follow them into battle and in a series of pitched battles, in which they were always an overwhelming minority, overthrew the power of the Syrian kings, captured Jerusalem and cleansed the temple. The day they cleansed the temple was named the Day of Dedication and it occurred on the 25th day of December. On that date Jews still celebrate the Feast of Dedication each year. The Maccabees, who were of the Asmonean family, began a line of high priests known as the Asmonean Dynasty. Their sons, for about the next three or four generations, ruled as priests in Jerusalem, all the time having to defend themselves against the constant assaults of the Syrian army who tried to recapture the city and the temple. During the days of the Maccabbees, there was a temporary overthrow of foreign domination which is why the Jews look back to this time and regard it with such tremendous veneration.

During this time, one of the Asmonean priests made a league with the rising power in the West; Rome. He signed a treaty with the Senate of Rome, providing for help in the event of Syrian attack. Though the treaty was made in all earnestness and sincerity, it was this pact which introduced Rome into the picture and history of Israel.

As the battles between the two opposing forces waged hotter and hotter, Rome was watchful.

Finally, the Governor of Idumea, a man named Antipater and a descendant of Esau, made a pact with two other neighboring kings and attacked Jerusalem to try to overthrow the authority of the Asmonean high priest. This battle raged so fiercely that finally Pompey, the Roman general, who happened to have an army in Damascus at the time, was besought by both parties to come and intervene. One side had a little more money than the other and persuaded by that logical argument, Pompey came down from Damascus, entered the city of Jerusalem; again with terrible slaughter, overthrew the city and captured it for Rome. That was in 63 B.C. From that time on, Palestine was under the authority and power of Rome.

Now Pompey and the Roman Senate appointed Antipater as the Procurator of Judea and he in turn made his two sons kings of Galilee and Judea. The son who became king of Judea is known to us a Herod the Great. ("Now when Jesus was born in Bethlehem of Judea in the days of Herod the king, behold, wise men from the East came to Jerusalem saying, "Where is he who has been born king of the Jews?"[1] (Matt. 2:1, 2 NKJV)

Meanwhile, the Pagan Empires around had been deteriorating and disintegrating. Their religions had fallen upon evil days. The people were sick of the *polytheism* and emptiness of their pagan faiths. The Jews had gone through times of pressure and had failed in their efforts to re-establish themselves and had given up all hope. There was a growing air of expectancy that the only hope they had left was the coming at last of the promised Messiah. In the East, the oriental empires had come to the place where the wisdom and knowledge of the past had disintegrated and they too were looking for something. When the moment came when the star arose over Bethlehem, the wise men of the East who were looking for an answer to their problems saw it immediately and came out to seek the One it pointed to. Thus, "when the time had fully come, God sent forth his Son."

It is amazing how God utilizes history to work out his purposes. Though we are living in the days that might be termed "the silence of God," when for almost 2,000 years there has been no inspired voice from God, we must look back, even as they did during those 400 silent years, upon the inspired record and realize that God has already said all that needs to be said, through the Old and New Testaments. God's purposes have not ended, for sure. He is working them out as fully now as he did in those days. Just as the world had come to a place of hopelessness then and the One who would fulfill all their hopes came into their midst, so the world again is facing a time when despair is spreading widely across the earth. Hopelessness is rampant everywhere and in this time God is moving to bring to fulfillment all the prophetic words concerning the coming of his Son again into the world to establish his kingdom. How long? How close? Who knows? But, what God has done in history he will do again, as we approach the end of "the silence of God."

Prayer:

Our Father, we are constantly encouraged as we see the fact that our faith is grounded upon historic things; that it touches history on every side. It is integrally related to life.

We pray that our own faith may grow strong and be powerful as we see the despair around us, the shaking of foundations, the changing of that which has long been taken to be permanent, the overthrowing of empires and the rising of others. Lord, we are thankful that we may look to you and realize that you are the One who does not change. Your Word is Eternal. As the Lord Jesus himself said, "Heaven and earth shall pass away, but my word shall not pass away." (Matthew 24:35 KJV) We pray in Christ's name, Amen.[9]

---

[9] Ray C. Stedman, "The 400 Years between the Old and New Testaments," *Adventuring through the Bible* (Discovery Publishing, 1995). https://www.raystedman.org/bible-overview/adventuring/the-400-years-between-the-old-and-new-testaments.

CHAPTER 7

Purpose and Significance of the Synagogue

Worship during the Intertestamental Period

Prior to the first Christian century, Judaism began to develop traditional interpretations of the Law that would eventually be written down to regulate Jewish life and worship. Judaism was influenced by Greek culture, resulting in the rise of a class of scribes and segments of the Jewish community that were more thoroughly Hellenized. The grouping formed during this period set the stage for the various sectarian movements within Judaism of the early Christian era.

The second temple in Jerusalem was the heart of Judaism in the first century. It was not only the religious center, but it functioned as a focus for national life and as a national reminder that God's hand was upon Israel. These functions made it the most important building in Israel. It was first the center of worship for the people of Israel. The temple was the divine dwelling place of God, and so it set Israel apart as the only nation where God chose to live.

The design of the temple was considered to represent the entire universe. Here was the place where Yahweh (the Lord) lived and ruled, a building ordained by God Himself.

The temple was the center for the study and teaching of the Torah, the second part of an unbreakable whole. It was here that the priesthood gained their significance, and from here they gained their provision.[10]

The temple took up 25 percent of the area of Jerusalem, architecturally. The design, emphasizing the importance of holiness and separation, drew one through progressive levels of purity, gradually excluding all but the high priest himself. It was heavily guarded to ensure the impure were kept away.

Politically, the ruler of the temple was the most important figure outside of the Roman governors. This made it an important focus for political parties, such as the Pharisees and Sadducees.

The third temple was built by King Herod. Distrust existed among some sections of Judaism, such as the Essenes, because the temple should have been built by a successor to Solomon. This combined with objections to the Hasmonean priesthood from the Pharisees, a political appointment by the Romans. There is little evidence of direct opposition to the temple.

The Jews respected the temple. They paid the temple tax gladly and brought their dedicatory offerings and tithes as they came to receive forgiveness and reintegration into the spiritual life of the nation. For the common Jew, it was the focus of pilgrimages and the center for the major feasts of the Jewish calendar. It also served as the nation's main slaughterhouse.

Earliest Examples of the Synagogue

The earliest examples of synagogue may be found as prayer houses in Egypt. They began to appear in Palestine some time after the Hasmonean era. They were meeting places, allowing like-minded people to gather together for a variety of functions focused, but not exclusively, on the study of the Torah, worship, and prayer.

The word *synagogue* can mean a building or refer to a community of people who built and used a building. The Jewish names for the synagogue indicate it was a "gathering place, a place of study and a court of law." The synagogue also functioned as a multifaceted community center. Funds were collected, both for charity and for the temple, and it was a banqueting house. It was a place of refuge and was used as a hostel for itinerants. It functioned as a center for social and political gatherings, and there is contested evidence that the synagogue in Sardis was given permission to perform sacrifices.

The synagogue of the first century gained its significance from the temple. Jews were often unable to visit the Temple as often as they would like, and so the synagogue became the next best alternative. It was here, then, that the Jewish festivals were celebrated and the Sabbath worship, tightly tied to the reading and teaching of the Torah, was conducted.[11]

---

[10] L. I. Levine, "The Second Temple Synagogue: The Formative Years," in *The Synagogue in Late Antiquity* (Philadelphia: ASOR, 1987), 14–19.
[11] E. P. Sanders, *Judaism: Practice and Belief 63 BCE-66 CE* (London: SCM Press, 1992), 52.

Architecturally, the synagogue was often a converted home or part of a larger structure designed for other purposes. The design inside was generally fairly plain, with little in the way of decoration or adornment. In Sardis, the synagogue is a part of a mammoth gymnasium complex.

There appeared to be less focus on purity than that found in the temple. It appears women were able to attend, as well as Gentiles and proselytes, and there was no requirement to attend, people only attending if they chose to. Diverse modes of worship were found, depending on where the synagogue was found.

We see that the temple was a national monument, commanding the national attention and reverence of the Jews and acting as a symbol of their election by God. In comparison, the synagogue was more of a utilitarian concept, functioning as a center for maintaining a specifically Jewish way of life for a more immediate province or community. Both the temple and the synagogue were religious in function but much more than that too. Where the temple was the center of religious worship and the teaching of the Torah, the synagogue provided worship and teaching to those unable to travel to the temple. Where the temple provided a focus for national political ambition, the synagogue served as a local center for meetings and discussion. Where the temple was the heart of the nation's socialization, the synagogue was the provincial heart of festivals and feasting.[32][12]

The synagogue is no less prominent than the temple in the gospel records. The custom of Jesus was to attend the synagogue on the Sabbath.

> And he came to Nazareth, where he had been brought up: and, as his custom was, he went into the synagogue on the sabbath day, and stood up for to read. (Luke 4:16 KJV)

In the synagogue at Nazareth, He read the prophetic passage and, in answer to the people's expectation, gave an astonishing exposition of it. In the first period of His ministry, He went about all Galilee, teaching in the synagogues.

> And Jesus went about all Galilee, teaching in their synagogues, and preaching the gospel of the kingdom, and healing all manner of sickness and all manner of disease among the people. (Matthew 4:23 KJV)

> And Jesus went about all the cities and villages, teaching in their synagogues, and preaching the gospel of the kingdom, and healing every sickness and every disease among the people. He cast out the unclean spirit in the synagogue at Capernaum. (Matthew 9:35 KJV)

---

[12] A. T. Kraabel, "The Diaspora Synagogue: Archaelogical and Epigraphic Evidence since Sukenik," in *Ancient Synagogues: Historical Analysis and Archaelogical Discovery*, eds. D. Urman & P. V. M. Flesher (Leiden: E.J. Brill, 1995), 102.

> And they went into Capernaum; and straightway on the sabbath day he entered into the synagogue, and taught And they were astonished at his doctrine: for he taught them as one that had authority, and not as the scribes. And there was in their synagogue a man with an unclean spirit; and he cried out, Saying, Let us alone; what have we to do with thee, thou Jesus of Nazareth? art thou come to destroy us? I know thee who thou art, the Holy One of God. And Jesus rebuked him, saying, Hold thy peace, and come out of him, And when the unclean spirit had torn him, and cried with a loud voice, he came out of him, And they were all amazed, insomuch that they questioned among themselves, saying, What thing is this? what new doctrine is this? for with authority commandeth he even the unclean spirits, and they do obey him. And immediately his fame spread abroad throughout all the region round about Galilee. (Mark 1:21–28 KJV)

He also faced the challenge of his opponents in the synagogue by healing the man with a withered arm on the Sabbath, and He warned His disciples that they would be scourged in the synagogues.

> And he entered again into the synagogue; and there was a man there which had a withered hand. And they watched him, whether he would heal him on the sabbath day; that they might accuse hint And he saith unto the man which had the withered hand, Stand forth. And he saith unto them, Is it lawful to do good on the sabbath days, or to do evil? to save life, or to kill? But they held their peace And when he had looked round about on them with anger, being grieved for the hardness of their hearts, he saith unto the man, Stretch forth thine hand. And he stretched it out: and his hand was restored whole as the other. (Mark 3:1–5 KJV)

> But beware of men: for they will deliver you up to the councils, and they will scourge you in their synagogues. (Matthew 10:17 KJV)

It seems that in the later stages of Jesus's ministry, although crowds still followed Him, He was no longer so welcome in the synagogues. Were not His followers put out of the synagogues as well?

> And great multitudes followed him; and he healed them there. (Matthew 19:2 KJV)

> These words spake his parents because they feared the Jews: for the Jews had agreed already, that if any man did confess that he was Christ, he should be put out of the synagogue. (John 9:22 KJV)

Nevertheless among the chief rulers also many believed on him; but because of the Pharisees they did not confess him, lest they should be put out of the synagogue. (John 12:42 KJV)

The Christian's relationship to the synagogue was equally strong, though the opportunity of exposition soon made the synagogue a place of contention and separation. Stephen, for example, seems to have engaged in synagogue evangelism, and Paul made the synagogue the starting point of his missionary work in the various cities, according to Acts 13. He preached in the synagogues at Pisidian, Antioch, and Iconium and found a house of prayer at Philippi. It was Paul's custom to attend the synagogue, and he reasoned for three Sabbaths in the synagogue, at Thessalonica.

Then there arose certain, of the synagogue, which is called the synagogue of the Libertines, and Cyrenians, and Alexandrians, and of them of Cilicia and of Asia, disputing with Stephen. And they were not able to resist the wisdom and the spirit by which he spake. (Acts 6:9–10 KJV)

Now when they had passed through Amphipolis and Apollonia, they came to Thessalonica where was a synagogue of the Jews: And Paul, as his manner was, went in unto them, and three sabbath days reasoned with them out of the scriptures. (Acts 17:1–2 KJV)

And when we came to Rome, the centurion delivered the prisoners to the captain of the guard: but Paul was suffered to dwell by himself with a soldier that kept him. (Acts 28:16 KJV)

Paul's detention probably prevented his worshiping at the synagogue and sought to persuade them of the truth of the gospel. In most of the Pauline churches, the first converts came from the synagogues, though in no instance did a whole synagogue become a Christian congregation.

The division that took place in the synagogues through the preaching of the gospel meant that Christians were forced to hold their own gatherings. They had been prepared for this by the special times of fellowship the first disciples had enjoyed with the Lord, whether formally at meals or more informally. The first church in Jerusalem met together in the upper room for prayer.

These all continued with one accord in prayer and supplication, with the women, and Mary the mother of Jesus, and with his brethren. (Acts 1:14 KJV)

> And when they had prayed, the place was shaken where they were assembled together; and they were all filled with the Holy Ghost, and they spake the word of God with boldness. (Acts 4:31 KJV)

> And when he had considered the thing, he came to the house of Mary the mother of John, whose surname was Mark; where many were gathered together praying. (Acts 12:12 KJV)

The breaking of bread, whether in the form of common meals, the Lord's Supper, or both, played some part in the movement toward the church's independent worship. Outside Jerusalem, Paul and Barnabas took steps to bring believers together for their own gatherings, which, in some instances, might have been supplementary to synagogue services, though there was a definite separation at Ephesus.

> But when divers were hardened, and believed not, but spake evil of that way before the multitude, he departed from them, and separated the disciples, disputing daily in the school of one Tyrannus. (Acts 19:9 KJV)

The pattern of worship already provided the conversion of leading members to help make the formation of Christian congregations a smooth and simple process. Believers met in houses, due to the absence of church buildings, and so you read of house churches, according to Philemon 2.

Developed after the pattern of the synagogue, the two chief ministers were the elder (bishop) and deacon. Prayer and the breaking of bread were primary. The meeting was on the first day of the week, on which the disciples broke bread and Paul preached. First Corinthians 11:23–34 speaks of a common meal, which is plainly the Lord's Supper, in combination with an ordinary supper. There was a gathering at which members might contribute a psalm, a doctrine, a tongue, a revelation, or an interpretation, with an emphasis on edifying and order.

Today, features of worship, include prayer, praise, exposition, reading of the scriptures, and the Lord's Supper. The materials of liturgy are also present. The psalms would be the Old Testament psalter, and the readings involved a fixed form of words. Paul gave us a simple order for the Lord's Supper. The sermons, recorded in Acts, are not without patent similarities of wording and structure. Since the primitive church is heir to the rich tradition of the Old Testament and Judaism, the new spirit and power lie in the new understanding of the old forms, the fashioning of new forms out of the old, rather than in formlessness.

E. Robert Webber, The Comulete Librae of Christian Worship, vol. 1. The Biblical Foundations of Christian Worship.

CHAPTER 8
Twentieth-Century Worship

The Praise-and-Worship Movement

A new style of worship has spread throughout North America and other parts of the world in the last several decades. This worship goes by several names; the most accepted is the praise-and-worship movement.

The praise-and-worship movement emerged from several trends in the sixties and early seventies. These trends indicated that traditional worship forms were dead. There was a concern for the immediacy of the Spirit, a desire for intimacy, a persuasion that music and informality must connect with people of a post-Christian culture.

In one of the earliest expressions, the rise of testimonial music was through the leadership of Bill Gaither in the early 1960s. Songs such as "He Touched Me," "There's Something about That Name," "Let's Just Praise the Lord," and "Because He Lives" touched many lives and introduced people to a new type of music. These songs were performance songs, but they soon became congregational; people sang along or joined in on the refrain.

In the late 1960s on the West Coast, a second expression of these trends came all over the world in the Jesus movement.[55] A major emphasis of this movement was the singing of praise choruses, some of which were written and sung as the congregation was at worship. Since those early days, this form of music and style of worship has developed into a worldwide approach to worship. The exact origins of the praise-and-worship tradition are not clear, but the movement itself is not difficult to describe. It seeks to recapture the lost element of praise found in both Old and New Testament worship.[13]

The proponents of praise and worship say, "Praise God first and foremost; then move on to the other elements of worship." A major feature of the praise-and-worship movement is its tendency to distinguish praise from worship. Judson Cornwall, a praise-and-worship leader in the movement and author of numerous books, makes the distinction between praise and worship in his book, *Let Us Worship*. He cites Psalm 95 as a distinction. In the opening verses, the psalmist invites praise.

> Come, let us sing for joy to the Lord; let us shout aloud to the rock of our salvation. Let us come before him with thanksgiving, and extol him with music and song. For the Lord is the great God, the great King above all gods. In his hand are the depths of the earth, and the mountain peaks belong to him. The sea is his, for he made it, and his hands formed the dry land. Come, let us bow down in worship, let us kneel before the Lord our Maker; for he is our God and we are the people of his pasture, the flock under his care. (Psalm 95:1–7 NIV)

Cornwall writes, "Praise prepares us for worship; it is a prelude to worship." Praise is not an attempt to get something from God; it is a ministry that we offer to God. We offer praise for what God has done, for God's mighty deeds in history, and His continued providential presence in our lives.

While we praise God for what He has done; we worship God for who He is. One praises highly the acts of God; the other praises the person and character of God.

The Temple Sequence

The order of service—the swing from praise to worship—is patterned after the movement in the Old Testament tabernacle and temple, from the outer court to the inner court and then into the holy of holies. These steps are accomplished through songs. The worship leader moves the congregation through the various steps that lead to worship.

The chorus begins with personal experience or testimony, such as, "This Is the Day the Lord Has Made" or "We Bring Sacrifices of Praise into the House of the Lord." These upbeat songs are centered on praise and relate to the personal experience of the believer.

In the tabernacle setting, people are still outside the fence that surrounds the tabernacle. They

---

[13] Robert E. Webber, *The Complete Library of Christian Worship*, vol. II. The Biblical Foundations of Christian Worship.

cannot worship until they come through the gates, into the tabernacle court. In the second step, the mood and the content of the music shift to express the action of entering the gates and coming into the courts. The worship leader leads people in songs that express the transition from praise to worship. These are songs of thanksgiving, such as Psalm 100, a psalm of praise.

> Make a joyful noise unto the Lord, all ye lands. Serve the Lord with gladness: come before his presence with singing. Know ye that the Lord he is God: it is he that hath made us, and not we ourselves; we are his people, and the sheep of his pasture. Enter into his gates with thanksgiving, and into his courts with praise: be thankful unto him, and bless his name. For the Lord is good; his mercy is everlasting; and his truth endureth to all generations. (Psalm 100:1–5 KJV)

The third step is into the holy of holies, which brings believers away from themselves and into a fully conscious worship of God alone. No longer is the worshipper thinking about what God has done but rather of who God is, in person and character. A quiet devotion hovers over the congregation as they sing songs such as "Father, I Adore You," "I Love You, Lord," and "You Are Worthy." Clapping will likely be replaced with devotional responses of upturned faces, raised hands, tears, and even a subtle change in the timbre of the voices. This is described as an experience of "the manifest presence of God."

This experience does not differ greatly from the liturgical experience of the presence of Christ at the Lord's Table. In this atmosphere the charismata (spiritual gifts) are released, and many today taste the special manifestations of the Holy Spirit in worship renewal, as he or she inhabits the praises of His people, according to Psalm 22:3: "But thou art holy, O thou that inhabitest the praises of Israel" (KJV).

Variations

The tabernacle/temple order of worship is quite noticeable in praise-and-worship churches; it is not the only order of sequence of song. The Vineyard Church in Anaheim, California, is a church that fits into the broader category of the praise-and-worship tradition of worship. It has a slightly different variation of the progression that brings a worshipper into God's presence.

The Vineyard Church worship begins with an invitation phase, which is like a call to worship, with songs of invitation such as "I Just Came to Praise the Lord." These may be sung with clapping, swinging the body, and looking at other worshippers, smiling, and acknowledging their presence.

In the next movement, the engagement phase, the people are brought closer to God, and their songs are addressed to Him, not to one another. An example may be "Humble Yourself in the Sight of the Lord."

The song leader moves the people into the adoration phase. The broad range of pitch and melody that characterized the previous phases is exchanged for the smaller range of music and the more subdued tone of songs such as "Jesus, Jesus, There's Something About That Name" or "Father, I Adore You."

The congregation is then led into the intimacy phase, which is the quietest and most personal part of the worship. Songs such as "O Lord, You're Beautiful" and "Great Are You, Lord" are personal statements of an intimate relationship directed from the believer to the Lord. Through these songs, people become highly intense and lose themselves in the ecstasy of the moment. People may stand with their heads and hands turned upward and eyes closed as they sing. John Wimber calls it "lovemaking to God." Some people kneel or even prostrate themselves on the floor during this quiet time.

The final phase of the worship progression is a close-out song; a song that helps the people move out of the experience of being transfixed on God to prepare for the next segment of the service, the time of teaching.

Praise, Worship, Teaching, Prayer, and Ministry

The most distinction of a typical service is in that of praise from worship. Some acts in the service include the time for teaching, intercessory prayer, and ministry. Most praise-and-worship churches are informal. The various acts of the service are done in an informal way. Teaching may end with a time of brief feedback or discussion, depending of the size of the congregation.

Intercessory prayer may be informal. A prayer circle may replace the traditional pastoral prayer. Many churches may enter a time of ministry. There, people are sent into various rooms, where those who are gifted with ministry for a particular need lay hands on them and pray.

What is experienced in this setting can be very meaningful, ministering in a powerful way to the people of God.

Response to Praise and Worship

Traditional churches have responded to the spread of praise and worship in three ways:

1. They have not responded at all (perhaps unaware or ignorant of the movement).
2. They are more aware of the praise-and-worship traditions but are indifferent to them or they actively dismiss them, arguing that they are "too superficial" or "too charismatic."
3. They are not only aware of praise and worship but seek to integrate this new approach to worship into local churches.

Holiness—Pentecostal Worship

Modem Pentecostalism began with the Azusa Street Revival of 1906 in Los Angeles. The Holy Spirit fell upon a group of worshippers and gifted them with the ability to speak in tongues. Modem Pentecostalism cannot be understood apart from its roots in the nineteenth-century Holiness movement. This movement traces its origin to John Wesley and to his conviction that a conversion experience should be followed by a second work of God's grace.

Some American Methodists insisted that a second work of sanctifying grace should be a part of everyone's Christian experience. The people who sought this holiness experience gathered in camp meetings to hear teaching, sing, and, through agonizing prayer, break through to the second work of grace.

Eventually, this movement produced new denominations known as the Church of the Nazarene, the Free Methodists, the Wesleyan Church, and the Christian and Missionary Alliance. These groups were known as movements that desired an intense religious experience in worship during the nineteenth century. The camp meetings were characterized by spontaneous freedom in worship, accompanied by shouting when they "broke through" and experienced sanctifying grace. People would weep and wail, groan out loud, and enter a near-convulsive state as they sought God.

When the Pentecostalism emerged in the early part of the twentieth century, it drew heavily on the convictions and experience of the Holiness movement. The Pentecostals drew their music lyrics and formed songs from the Holiness movement.

Worship among Pentecostals, like that of their predecessors, was characterized by freedom, spontaneity, individual expression, and joy.

In its beginning, worship was not corporate as much as it was a corporate gathering for the purpose of simultaneous individual praise and worship. This gave the worship of Pentecostalism, in the mind of some, disorder and chaos. One strong characteristic of early Pentecostal worship was its singing and music. From the beginning, it used its cultural music to present the gospel. These songs tell stories of how people came to faith and received Jesus.

Some of these songs were "I Came to Jesus, Weary, Worn, and Sad" and "He Took My Sins Away." Some songs were seen as given by the Holy Spirit to a particular person, and some were found in the repertoire of churches, locally and around the world.

Pentecostalism has introduced a wide variety of musical instruments into its worship, including the pipe organ, guitar, drums, stringed instruments, and synthesizers. Many Pentecostal churches have a full orchestra that accompanies soloists, supports congregational singing, and performs sacred music.

Another feature of Pentecostal worship is praying and singing in the Spirit. This kind of prayer is more than Spirit-directed prayer; it is an actual Spirit-given language known as tongues. Tongues may occur in two different forms:

1. In some cases, a message may be given in tongues. During this time, a hush falls over the congregation, and everyone listens to the messages in tongues. It is followed by interpretation, through which the message given by God in another language is communicated in the language of the people.

2. A second form is manifested when everyone is praying out loud, many in a prayer language that is understood only by God. In these times of prayer, directed by the worship leader or occurring spontaneously after a song, no interpretation is made, for tongues in this instance is not a message from God but a personal "prayer language."[14]

Prophecies are also a unique feature of Pentecostal worship. A prophecy is a short message given by a person for the purpose of strengthening, encouraging, or comforting the worshipper. According to 1 Corinthians 14:3, "But the one who prophesies speaks to people for their strengthening, encouraging and comfort" (NIV).[15]

---

[14] Winters, Mary R. Reports taken from *Worship Old and New,* Robert E. Webber, "Worship Renewal in the Twentieth Century," 2003.

[15] *The Layman's Parallel Bible, New Revised Standard* (The Zondervan Corporation, 1991).

CONCLUSION

Evolution has been defined as the "development of life from lower to higher forms." According to the *Oxford Dictionary*, "Science is a branch of study which is concerned either with a connected body of demonstrated truths or with observed facts systematically classified. They're more or less collected by being brought under general laws and includes trustworthy methods for the discovery of new truth within its own domain."

However; from the perspective of Christian worship and the evolution of it, the pattern of worship, historically, calls for a divine response. It is a meeting with God in which the eternal covenant is affirmed in worship.

When God appeared to the Hebrews to give them the Law, it was an awesome sight. There were tremendous thunder-and-lightning storms. Mount Sinai was covered with smoke that billowed into the sky like a furnace. The whole mountain shook with a violent earthquake, and God commanded the people not to come near the mountain, "lest they die."

God is a holy God, and He was about to reveal Himself to His covenant people. Already, they had been murmuring and complaining. Parties to a covenant, however, cannot walk together unless they are in agreement.

In the beginning, God created a perfect universe that was orderly and harmoniously operated within His will. But man chose to rebel against God's will. Man's rebellion brought chaos and destruction on him and everything around him. Look around us; we can realize this truth!

God's Plan

God's plan says,

> Although the penalty for sin is death, you don't have to pay it. I'll come to earth and pay it for you. I'll purchase your salvation with my own blood. For the wages of sin is death; but the gift of God is eternal life through Jesus Christ our Lord. (Romans 6:23 KJV)

> In Him we have redemption through His blood, the forgiveness of sins, according to the riches of His grace" (Ephesians 1:7 NKJV)

This is God's provision. From the beginning, God determined that He would provide Himself with His own blood, as the evidence that the penalty had been paid.

> Forasmuch as ye know that ye were not redeemed with corruptible things, as silver and gold, from your vain conversation received by tradition from your fathers; But with the precious blood of Christ, as of a lamb without blemish and without spot: Who verily was foreordained before the foundation of the -world, but was manifest in these last times for you. (1 Peter 1:18–20 KJV)

God determined that, at a certain time in history, He would become the "Lamb of God" who takes away the sins of the world. When Adam and Eve sinned, they covered themselves with leaves and hid from God. It was their way of covering their sin. When God saw this, He knew it was time to explain the spiritual facts of life.

God killed an innocent animal and accepted its blood as a substitute and a temporary covering of their sin. Although it was an imperfect substitute, it would point everybody in the right direction.

Adam and Eve became proud parents of two sons, Cain and Abel. Cain, being the oldest, took up farming as a livelihood. Abel was a shepherd. Adam taught his children about the blood covenant.

> And in process of time it came to pass, that Cain brought of the fruit of the ground an offering unto the Lord. And Abel, he also brought of the firstlings of his flock and of the fat thereof. And the Lord had respect unto Abel and to his offering. (Genesis 4:3–4 KJV)

God approved Abel's offering because this was the way He established for sinful man to approach Him; therefore, Abel was acceptable to God, based on the innocent blood sacrifice. Contrary to his younger brother, Cain rejected God's way. He rejected the blood covenant. Instead of bringing an innocent sacrifice, he brought the fruit of his own labor, although it probably was his very best. Although it's our very best, goodness cannot measure up to a perfect, absolute, holy God.

The covenant continued through Seth, Noah, Abraham, Isaac, and Jacob and then Moses. God, therefore, established a *sacrifice system*. The system would have five types of sacrifices. Each sacrifice would uniquely reveal something about the nature of the old covenant.

The five types of offerings were sin offering, trespass offering, burnt offering, meal offering, and peace offering. These offerings were to be the physical, outward expressions of the longings of the inward heart in seeking communion with God.

The sin offering and trespass offering were mandatory offerings associated with the sin of the nation and the individual Hebrew. The burnt offering, meal offering, and peace offering were spontaneous, voluntary offerings of praise and thanksgiving. They were not associated with the individual's sin but were part of his worship to God.

The New Covenant (from the Processional to the Recessional)

But in the fullness of time, God sent forth His Son, born of a woman, born as a Jew. All the fullness of God dwelled in Him.

> But when the fulness of the time was come, God sent forth his Son made of a woman, made under the law. (Galatians 4:4 KJV)

> For it pleased the Father that in him should all fulness dwell. (Colossians 1:19 KJV)

> For in him dwelleth all the fulness of the Godhead bodily. (Colossians 2:9 KJV)

God was in Christ, reconciling the world unto Himself. God had come to earth in the man Jesus Christ to pay the penalty for sin on our behalf. He came to purchase our salvation with His own blood.

Jesus Christ is the one for whom Adam and Eve were waiting. The skins of the innocent animals covering their bodies were a constant reminder that He would come. Jesus Christ is that more acceptable sacrifice, in whom Abel put his trust. Jesus Christ is the substitute offering that renewed the covenant with Seth and his descendants. Jesus Christ is Noah's sacrifice, which moved God to put a rainbow in the sky. Jesus Christ is the one Abraham believed in and was counted as righteous. Jesus Christ is the reason God was the God of Abraham, Isaac, and Jacob. Jesus Christ is Moses's sacrifice before Pharaoh. Jesus Christ is the new covenant sacrifice that takes away the sins of the world. He is the one to which the old covenant sacrifices pointed so that everyone would recognize Him when He arrived on the scene.

Worship Is a Person

When Jesus gave Himself as the perfect sacrifice, He fulfilled the old covenant. We no longer worship a system but a person. Jesus Christ is that person, and He is the sacrifice needed for cleansing.

Speaking of Himself through King David, God said,

> Sacrifice and offering thou didst not desire; mine ears hast thou opened: burnt offering and sin offering hast thou not required. Then said I, Lo, I come (in the volume of the book it is written of me). (Psalm 40:6–7 KJV)

> For it is not possible that the blood of bulls and of goats should take away sins. Wherefore when he cometh into the world, he saith, Sacrifice and offering thou wouldest not, but a body hast thou prepared me: In burnt offerings and sacrifices for sin thou hast had no pleasure. Then said I, Lo, I come (in the volume of the book it is written of me,) to do thy will, 0 God. Above when he said, Sacrifice and offering and burnt offerings and offering for sin thou wouldest not, neither hadst pleasure therein; which are offered by the law; Then said he, Lo, I come to do thy will, O God. He taketh away the first, that he may establish the second. By the which will we are sanctified through the offering of the body of Jesus Christ once for all. (Hebrews 10:4–10 KJV)

Both Jew and Gentile may enter into the new covenant through the blood of Jesus, the once-and-for-all perfect sacrifice.

The Setting of Worship in Contemporary Churches

There is a reconfiguration of the worship space through the new shifts that are taking place in worship today. Underneath these shifts is the biblical understanding of worship that has been recovered as the congregational celebration of God's mighty deeds of salvation.

Worship was no longer something to be watched or listened to, but because of the coronavirus (COVID-19), confirmed January 20, 2020, in the United States, people have been observing ministry at home and having online services and small-group discussions at home. Churches have been shut down by the CDC (Centers for Disease Control and Prevention), due to COVID-19. The coronavirus has spread worldwide. In the midst of confusion and fear, there's even more reason to get in the presence of God for praise and worship.

I've discovered that praise and worship still require us to give God adoration and praise with thanksgiving. It still requires us to sings songs, to have our own personal prayers, and to lay prostrate before the Lord, crying out to God to make sense of a world we have never known. Many church doors are closed and are now having virtual services. We find ourselves spending more time with God in praise and worship to seek answers. Some say, "This is the new normal." We find ourselves going to our prayer closets for church and calling the order of worship in our living rooms and making them our sanctuaries. Praise and worship are still something we can do in the lifting of our hands toward heaven, especially during this pandemic. But the position of worship has not changed because God still expects us to show up. The leaders of our churches still expect us to return to a brick-and-mortar worship center.

The first shift is from a preacher-dominated worship to a people-centered worship. Protestant worship has been a preacher-dominated worship. The people have been arranged in rows, directed toward the platform. The platform is directed toward the congregation. In this space, the preacher is often seen as the program director or the teacher. The people are there for the instruction or the "show."

The second shift is the return of worship to the people (liturgy: "work of the people"), which changes worship. This, in turn, creates the need to restructure worship space. You might have noticed that worship is experiencing a shift in music from an organ-dominated sound to the sound of a variety of musical instruments, including strings, basses, synthesizers, pianos, guitars, and drums. Churches now must take into account the need for band space—in some cases, space for a full orchestra.

The shifting row of the choir demands a reconsideration of worship space. The choir that once played the role of performer is now moving into the role of cantor and musical leader for the entire congregation. This is the new choir. Adequate space is needed for the choir, processions, and seating. Side seating facilitates involvement with the congregation, rather than front seating. The front seating implies performance.

Another shift taking place in worship is the increased celebration of the sacraments in Sunday worship. This is the weekly Eucharist, toward the celebration of baptism in worship; the anointing of oil for healing necessitates a new consideration of spatial arrangement.

Finally, many churches have introduced a time of ministry in worship that necessitates new spatial considerations. If they invite people to come forward for prayer, for the laying on of hands, and for other kinds of ministry, they need adequate space for these functions of worship ministry.

The kind of space that seems adequate to this new approach to worship is a centralized space, rather than the longitudinal space. Centralized space brings people into the action of worship and allows their worship to be considerably more participatory than longitudinal space.

Space needs to be redemptive space. It needs to reflect the work of salvation, which we celebrate. Therefore, adequate space for gathering, for the hearing of the Word, for the celebration of the Eucharist, and for music and arts that accompany these acts is a priority.

Christians do proclaim, by word and rite, Christ's death and Resurrection, and they respond in faith with praise and thanksgiving. This is why worship necessitates forms and signs.

BIBLIOGRAPHY

Annie's "Yom Kippur" Page.

Bunty, Paul and David Collins.

Conner, Kevin J. *The Tabernacle of David*. City Bible Publishing, 1976.

Conner, Kevin J. *The Tabernacle of Moses*. City Bible Publishing, 1976.

Conner, Kevin J. *The Temple of Solomon*. City Bible Publishing, 1976.

"Day of Atonement," Encarta Online.

Dolphin, Lambert. "Temple of Solomon." http://ldolphin.org.

Habershon, Ada R. *The Study of the Types*. Grand Rapids, MI: Kregel Publications, year.

Kappil, Joseph. "The Rise and Fall of Temple of Jerusalem," Through the Homeland of Jesus. http://www.Datanumeric.com/vlm/10-98/23.html.

Kraabel, A. T. "The Diaspora Synagogue: Archaelogical and Epigraphic Evidence since Sukenik." In *Ancient Synagogues: Historical Analysis and Archaeological Discovery*, edited by D. Urman and P. V. M. Flesher. Leiden: E. J. Brill, 1995.

Leoh, Dr. Vincent. "Fulfilling God's Destiny for Your Life." April 2001.

Levine, L. I., "The Second Temple Synagogue: The Formative Years." In *The Synagogue in Late Antiquity*, edited by L. I. Levine. Philadelphia: ASOR, 1987.

Nelson's Topical Bible Index. Nashville: Thomas Nelson, 1997. electronic edition,

New International Version of the Bible, King James Version, New King James Version, the Living Bible, the Amplified Bible, and the Message. New York International Bible Society.

Sanders, E. P. *Judaism: Practice and Belief 63 BCE–66 CE*. London: SCM Press, 1992.

Solomon, Steckoll. *The Temple Mount*. London: Tom Stacey Ltd., 1972.

Stedman, Ray C. "The 400 Years between the Old and New Testaments," *Adventuring through the Bible*. Discovery Publishing, 1995. https://www.raystedman.org/bible-overview/adventuring/the-400-years-between-the-old-and-new-testaments.

Taylor, Gardner C. "Seeing Our Hurts with God's Eyes." *Essential Taylor* CD. Hampton Minister's Conference, 1991.

The Holy Bible, King James Version. World Bible Publishers, 1974.

The Layman's Parallel Bible, KJV, NIV, and New Revised Standard. Zondervan Corporation, 1991.

"The Second Temple, Zerubbabel's Temple—'Desecrated and ransacked, but not destroyed and torn down.'" http://www.endtimeinfo.net/temple/whichtemple.html.

Webber, Robert E. *The Complete Library of Christian Worship*, vol. I and II. Peabody, MA: Hendrickson Publishers, 1996.

Webber, Robert E. *Worship Old and New.* City: Publisher, 2003.

Webster's New World Dictionary. Williams Collins Publisher, Inc., 1979.

World Book Encyclopedia.

Printed in the United States
by Baker & Taylor Publisher Services